ALONG MY FATHER'S HILLS

NOW MID-MARCH OLD

Now Mid-March old, the year is greenly turning
The curve of Spring; along a hundred ways
I trace among the waking grass and bramble
The soundless steps of days.

So sure she comes, though Northern winds defy her,
Mocking each footstep slow,
Tombing in ice her hollow fields and lowlands,
Cairning her heights with snow.

To-morrow she will laugh in many waters -
Ever the olden promise she fulfils -
To-morrow she will set the furze-bloom burning
Along my father's hills.

Michael Walsh

From: **MICHAEL WALSH** - Collected Poems, 1996

To celebrate the centenary of Michael Walsh - The Poet of Fore - born in 1897 and whose death in the winter of 1938 robbed Ireland of one of its purest and most authentic voices, I have gathered a selection of his essays, together with varied prose and poetry of his elder brother William. When Michael's first collection of poems "Brown Earth and Green" was published, he paid a tribute to his brother by writing a dedication across the title page: "To my brother Willie, to whose fine poetic taste and discrimination over long years, my pen owes much."

A journalist, a critic and student of poetry, and a poet in his own right, William Walsh - with his brother Michael - went to the National School of St. Fechin's, Fore, Co. Westmeath where their uncle was schoolmaster. Their love of literature was instilled into them by their father and grandfather.

Patrick Walsh

ACKNOWLEDGEMENT

To the Editors of The Irish Independent, The Irish Press, The Evening Herald, The Irish Catholic, The Standard, The Irish Rosary, The Father Mathew Record, Bonaventura, SVD Annual, thanks are due for kind permission to include here essays and poems originally contributed to their pages.

ALONG MY FATHER'S HILLS

A MISCELLANY
BY
MICHAEL & WILLIAM
WALSH

FOREWORD
BENEDICT KIELY

This collection published 1997 by
Patrick Walsh
65 Croydon Park Avenue, Dublin 3. Ireland.

FOR MAUREEN, HELEN
EITHNE & MARY

ISBN 0 9528293 1 2

Printed in Ireland by Colour Books Ltd., Dublin.

FOREWORD

It was in the Autumn of 1939, a year that will never be forgotten that in the house of Brian na Banban, Brian O'Higgins, poet and seagreen, incorruptible Irish patriot I first encountered a lovely, silverhaired lady. She was Teresa Brayton who had caught the heart of Ireland with "The Old Bog Road" and much more. We became friends. It was an honour to be in her company.

She invited me to call some evening to where she lived in Fairview; to meet some friends, she said, who turned out to be William Walsh and his son Paddy. We stepped immediately into everlasting friendship, cemented by their bringing me for my first visit to their enchanted Vale of Fore of the Seven Wonders.

William belonged there, or the Vale belonged to him and his memories. And I had already rejoiced in the poetry and prose of his brother, Michael, and I knew of Fore. But to be brought there by the poet's brother was a special honour.

That was the first of many visits to Fore. And it seemed natural that the journey should, by a festival, be made a permanent feature of life. And in strong friendships we visited other places in Ireland and on the mainland, and encountered many friends.

I was happy to introduce him to my elder brother and they met as if they had known each other in happiness in a previous life. William had that rare gift. You felt he had been there forever and thinking of you. And still when I say to myself some of the poems of Michael, I see William smiling there before me and beckoning me on into the Enchanted Valley.

Benedict Kiely

MICHAEL WALSH
Contents

WILLIAM WALSH
Contents

Dublin Literary Memories

These remain still at the root of my poetry - the reeds in the bog; summer coming in clouds of white daisies to the sloping fields at the back of the house, and the "hill of Ben" itself like some eternal symbol amid the suns and mist of change. Yet when I came to Dublin I soon learned to love its life and moods, its restless crowded thoroughfares - those ever-changing galleries of humanity. And it was a city that was not so very far from my childhood fields. The roundabout journey by train from Oldcastle via Drogheda seemed long, especially as the lights of Dublin loomed so near on very dark nights. From across the half-door I could see eastward in the inky sky a white glare. No doubt it was sixty miles away, but I knew that underneath it was Dublin. Sometimes I would think of Tennyson:-

"And my spirit leaped within me to be gone before me then
In beneath the lights I looked at, in among the throngs of men"

From the same half-door in daylight I could see the grey-blue outline of the Wicklow mountains. Their faint dream-like distance allured. From my father's higher fields one could see that far-off entire range of mountains - calm with a seeming tranquillity that was not of this world. Those lower slopes northward where the wandering peaks ended were the dim Dublin hills.

Before I came to the city to employment in a publishing house, I had followed in the newspapers the doings of literary Dublin. One day I saw an announcement of a coming debate in the Abbey Theatre in which G.K. Chesterton would take part. I wanted to see Chesterton in the life - not so much the doughty champion of sanity in a world gone awry - as the poet of Don John of Austria. So on a sunlit October morning, when I had dug the day's potatoes, I set forth on a newly-purchased second-hand bicycle, and in this way linked up for the first time my Westmeath Ben-of-Fore with Nelson Pillar.

Sometimes there is a sense of disappointment when we turn from a man's writings to see or meet the author himself. I think it will be agreed that all who have seen and heard G.K.C. went back to his books newly enriched. As I saw him seated by a table on the Abbey stage, his gargantuan proportions - that were a source of amusement even to himself - seemed to be the just ally to the giant equipment of his mind. One noted, too, the indifference of genius to those sartorial details that attract the superficial eye. Meticulousness - in having one's tie at just the precise angle; one's clothes creased in tailor's dummy fashion - such starch-board decorum would be in conflict with that refreshing air of freedom that was G.K.C.

As he listened to Mr. Thomas Johnson lead off the debate, he seemed to chuckle good-humouredly to himself over points which he would challenge by and by. Presently he brought to light from some of the recesses of his pockets an enormous pencil. Almost a miniature baton. I remember once seeing a carpenter with such a pencil. And now when he produced an equally enormous penknife and commenced pointing the great pencil, a wave of half-suppressed laughter ran through the audience. He made a few notes. The subject of the debate was: "Is Private Property Necessary to the Welfare of Mankind ?" Mr. Johnson spoke trenchantly in defence of co-operative ownership. Chesterton, with inimitable wit, paradox and logic, advocated private property. His effectiveness of speech lay in his manner of hesitating; and in his slow deliberation. If he spoke rapidly, time would not have been allowed to get to the depth of his utterances. A literary friend of mine wondered if this verbal hesitancy was not cultivated, since it enlisted concentrated attention to what was about to be said next ? It was a night of sparkling retort. I saw and heard Bernard Shaw for the first time; earlier in the evening I had recognised the long back of his head from the Rodin sculpture. Mr. Yeats, looking every inch a poet, slowly and vaguely surveyed the audience, or was he merely gazing far beyond it into the days of Ossian and hearing somewhere in the depths of his consciousness the echoes of his own song:-

"And we rode on the plains of the sea's edge
- the sea's edge barren and gray,
Gray sands on the green of the
grasses and over the dripping trees,

9

Dripping and doubling landward as though they would hasten away
Like an army of old men longing for rest from the moan of the
seas."

Perhaps he was !

The long Yeats forelock is as famous as the Shavian beard. When the discussion closed, there were many questions; everybody was clamouring to get Shaw to his feet. A dozen questions were hurled at him from all sides of the house - from the stalls, from the pit, from the gallery. What amazed me was his memory for the bombardment of questions; he singled them out rapidly and with words that came tersely, and like machine-gun fire, he answered each interrogation, if not always to the satisfaction of the individual, at least to the general entertainment of the house. There was no air of opulence about Shaw, even though a short manuscript of his was worth a thousand golden guineas. His athletic vitality; his short tight-fitting jacket suggested an efficient little tradesman ready to do a job of work and do it well.

While such Dublin nights of debate were all too rare, the city within the last quarter of a century has had many literary societies. In the mid-War years there was the Bookman's Club which scanned the weekly periodicals in search of young poets. I do not think their quest was rewarded by the discovery of even one authentic singer ! The National Literary Society brought together many of Ireland's leading poets, writers and scholars. Dr. George Sigerson was a familiar figure. So was the present President of Eire - Dr. Douglas Hyde. It was there also I first heard Daniel Corkery lecture on the Big House of the Eighteenth Century - a paper that afterwards found permanent form in his "Hidden Ireland". It was the night of the Corkery lecture that D.L. Kelleher told of a prophecy he had made twenty years before. He had predicted the success of the young man who had now justified his prophecy both as a playwright and as a master of fiction. Corkery had written that strangely arresting and memorable book, "A Munster Twilight," which was hailed at home and abroad as a literary masterpiece and a transcript from life. There was also the Dublin Literary Society. Was it here or at the National I heard Darrel Figgis lecture on some aspect of English literature ? He looked curiously foreign with his short flaming beard; but he was a charming lecturer speaking with a swift magnetic enthusiasm and without notes.

I was in at the beginning of no less than three of Dublin's Literary Clubs. The earliest with which I was associated was *St. Enda's*. The Aran Saint, to whose memory Pearse's school was dedicated, also inspired the title of a young people's journal which Brian O'Higgins founded and edited. Our Club took its name from this *"St. Enda's"*.

We talked over our programme in the Nallys' beautiful home in Rathmines. A member of this patriotic western family was Dr. T.W. Nally, who wrote something that was off the beaten path of Jack and the Beanstalk - an Irish pantomime. Written in English and entitled, "Finn Varra Ma," it was produced at the Theatre Royal and was a great success. Why is it not revived ? I remember the late Dr. Nally telling me about a play of his which was in rehearsal at the Abbey when the Rising of 1916 took place. It was called, " The Spancel of Death," and was, I believe, a grim prophetic play. Thus crisis and upheaval can dislocate the world of art; and now I think of Brinsley MacNamara telling me with smiling stoicism of the sole MS. of the only book with which he was thoroughly satisfied. On its way to the London publisher it got lost in the Irish Sea - having gone down in the *Leinster*. But to go back to our *St. Enda's Club*. Its founders were: Lilian Nally, whose delicate and sincere verse Brian O'Higgins has since published under "A Knapsack of Dreams"; M.M. Brennan, who wrote the Abbey comedy, "The Young Man From Rathmines". Mairin O'Kennedy, who was a contributor to *Banba* and *The Gael* - two ambitious journals which had a brilliant if short life in the momentous months of 1921; Padraig Horan, some of whose poems appeared in the English *Sunday Times;* M.J. Murray, of the *Evening Mail;* Eamon Kavanagh, a University student, and myself.

In the early spring of 1922 we held our first meeting at rooms in Castle Street. The birth of *"St. Enda' s Literary Club "* was announced in the morning papers, and a number of applications for membership arrived. Amongst those who looked in to see us at

11

Castle Street was the Gaelic author, Padraig Og O'Conaire. M.J. Murray, as Chairman or President, showed us what big things the Club could accomplish if only we co-operated and worked hard. In his view, the Society should not merely consist of debates and social evenings; we were to have a Literary or Press bureau through which articles, stories and poems could be submitted and syndicated abroad. Eilis Ni Riain, of Dundrum, then recently home from school in France, came to join us. Tall, dark-haired and with an air of pleasantness that added to her good looks, she had, too, a sense of literary art in advance of her years. Almost from the outset she had adopted the pen-name, "Deirdre O'Brien." and I must confess that in those days I foresaw the coming poet rather than the best-selling novelist whose name is now known to hundreds of thousands of readers throughout Great Britain and Ireland. This smiling, happy-hearted girl, who always gave the impression of carefreeness and leisure, astonished us by the countless pages of MS. she could write in a brief space of time. Serial followed serial with no sign of haste or lack of finish. The Ryans' home at Dundrum, with its great garden overlooking a stream towards the tall trees beyond, remains a bright springtide memory to the half-dozen or so who were the young literary Dublin of those years. A little way to the west were the mist-soft mountains that gave Deirdre O'Brien the title for her first and best novel, "Grey Hills for Dreams." It was at Ryans' I first met Miss Annie Smithson.

Padraig Horan and myself were both the advocates and defenders of the poets at those "*St. Enda's*" meetings. Some of the more mathematical-minded debaters took a delicious (or, should I say, malicious) delight in teasing us, demanding an analysis of our flights of fancy - a definition of poetry, as if indeed poetry by its very nature could ever be defined.

I remember one night Paddy Horan accompanied me part of the way homeward through the lamplit drizzle of the streets. His natural tide of eloquence, always stimulating, had a somewhat melancholy strain that night, as we discussed the average attitude to poets and their poetry. We were not old enough, I suppose, to laugh with the world at the poor poet and still remember that he was heir to riches unpurchasable by the dross of earth or time - a

12

divinely-illuminated heritage.

Like the character in Goldsmith, who came to scoff and remained to pray, a member of one of our audiences, who listened uncomprehendingly and unmoved to what I am about to quote, wrote to me years afterwards from a foreign country begging me to recall it and send it to him. The stanzas were from Francis Thompson's "In No Strange Land." Did my correspondent at last have a vision of the light that never was on sea or land ?

O world invisible, we view thee,
O world intangible, we touch thee,
O world unknowable, we know thee,
Inapprehensible, we clutch thee !

Does the fish soar to find the ocean,
The eagle plunge to find the air -
That we ask of the stars in motion
If they have rumour of thee there?
Not where the wheeling systems darken,
And our benumbed conceiving soars ! -
The drift of pinions, would we hearken,
Beats at our own clay-shuttered doors.

The angels keep their ancient places -
Turn but a stone, and start a wing
'Tis ye, 'tis your estranged faces
That miss the many-splendoured thing.

One day in Grafton Street, Eamon Kavanagh asked me what was the *St. Enda's Club* going to achieve by talk ? His voice was stern, and I felt that he would have us realize that the sword was mightier than the pen. The unhappy Civil War was looming. Some of the members shouldered rifles. Then the internment camp, while the skeleton *St. Enda's* that met subsequently in Eustace Street slowly and naturally dissolved.

True poetry should be read aloud, and the voice in which he speaks his poem is the infallible test of a poet. We had no public poetry readings in *St.Enda's Club* that I can recollect. Lilian Nally,

13

whose sponsor at baptism was none other than Ethna Carbery, could read a poem with a voice that created in the sympathetic listener an ethereal exaltation; her words brought forth all the enchantment and haunting wonder of the poem.

No European city has in its surroundings so much to offer the lover of long walks as Dublin. Even when the ferns of Mount Pelier and Three Rock burn red and copper in the October light, the little hill roads above Rathfarnham lure you 'way and away. One Sunday in autumn, many years ago, I took one of those circuitous rambles with a novelist and a poet. We had tea in a white, mountain cottage, where hot buttered scones give such satisfying completeness to an afternoon's long climbing walk. The writer was towering, broad-shouldered and kindly Brinsley MacNamara, and the poet a generously-built man, too - broad-hatted, bespectacled, Yeatsian-looking F.R. Higgins. It was then I first heard of the newly-formed Circle of Literature and the Arts - the Radical Club. Brinsley told F.R. that as a journalist I was eligible for membership; anyhow, I was welcome to come to the next meeting, and then I could decide.

In a large room - (I am open to correction, for it may have been Dawson Street and not Frederick Street) - that in its tones and colours responded to the newest notions in art, many people had gathered. They talked here and there in groups. Poets, playwrights, lawyers, actors, painters - I recognised many faces. A lithe, fair, blue-eyed young man, with something of a challenge in his voice, kept a whole bench enlivened with his animated speech. I had never seen him before. Presently we were introduced. His name was Liam O'Flaherty. I knew then that a writer so alien to my thought and ideals could not be a member of the Club which I visualized - a Circle that would represent a literature mirroring the sweetness, the serenity, and the normal way of Irish life.

There was a debate or discussion on the word "Culture". What did it mean ? Various definitions of culture were essayed - some of them arrestingly individual. Liam O'Flaherty was all out for fistic culture, the defending of one's convictions with the fists. I forget in what connection Mr. Alex Lynn, B.L., spoke so

14

engagingly on culture as expressed in the fosterage of a garden vegetable - a head of cabbage, for example.

When the exchanges of opinion later more directly concerned literature, I could have applauded M.J. MacManus for the plain commonsense of his remarks regarding the novels of Annie M.P. Smithson. It showed that he was not obsessed with abnormality in art or highbrow extremes. Tea was served; there were charades and folk-songs, and there was a futuristic touch about the crayon drawings that hung upon the walls. Liam O'Flaherty would have the Radical Club open to everybody - I remember that he specially mentioned Parish Priests, whether in sincerity or as a sneer I could not be sure. Though the entertainment was varied, and there were many likeable people there, I felt that the Radical Club was not the literary circle in which I would feel most at home. I did not go to any of its subsequent meetings.

I am not throwing bouquets around indiscriminately when I say that Father Stephen Brown, S.J., is one of the most important men of letters in the Ireland of this century. Why ? you will ask. He has not written any novels ? No. Nor volumes of essays ? Not exactly. But if you have read even a small number of those articles on cultural or social subjects of the hour which have appeared above his name in the Catholic Reviews you will readily agree that a more sane, a more lucid, and a more effective pen is not to be found in the hand of any critic of life and letters writing to-day. He is in touch with the trend of journalism and literature on both sides of the Atlantic.; he is a specialist in the domain of Catholic literature, while his bibliographical volumes also show how exhaustively he has covered the home field of Irish fiction. With sympathy and understanding he has got to the heart of poetry, while his writings on imagery - especially the imagery of the Bible - are proof that some of the world's best poets - paradoxical though it may sound - have never written a poem ! His sentences have the clarity, the balance, and the simplicity that characterise the phrasing of the best essayists like E.V. Lucas or Robert Lynd. And it need scarcely be added that it is in the light of Catholic thought and philosophy he reviews every subject that engages his pen. He can see at once through artistic pose and sham, and he has broken a lance even with *"AE"* over the list of names that the *"Irish Statesman"* was continually calling forth as representative of Irish literature - the O'Flahertys, the O'Caseys and the Dunsanys. And thus I come to another of Dublin's literary societies of past years - the Catholic Writer's Guild. It was at its meetings I realized the asset that Father Brown could be to any Catholic Writers' Circle - his helpful criticism, his suggestions, his advice would prove invaluable.

I was associated with the founding of this Guild, and I hope that at some new date, somebody - maybe, indeed, the Editor of BONAVENTURA - will form a new Catholic Circle of Literature so strong that its influence will be felt outside Ireland. In time it might have its own Radio and its own system of distributing truly representative Irish books throughout other countries.

The members of the Executive of this Guild of other days had duties that called them away - some of them out of the country. But they were prepared to make many sacrifices. Their enthusiasm was infectious, and indeed finally had not the Committee been thus scattered - one of its ablest journalist-members took up an editorial post in England - I think this Catholic Society of Letters would still be flourishing.

And we had mustered about us writers of whom any Literary Circle would be proud. T.C. Murray, one of whose plays at that time was taking London by storm; L.S. Gogan, of the National Museum, the Gaelic poet; J.H. Cox - who remembers this tall, stately man with the grey, serious, sympathetic eyes, whose human and witty commentaries were a widely-read feature of both the *Sunday* and *Daily Independent* ? And yet this was but a recreation for J.H.C. of the *Irish Independent*. The writer of "To-Day and Yesterday" was a valued and efficient officer in the Department of Agriculture. And speaking of the *Independent,* our Circle could boast some of its able contributors, even he who afterwards became its Editor-in-Chief - Mr. T.A. Quilty; Miss Gertrude Gaffney, Miss Deirdre O'Brien, Hugh P. Allen, Maurice R. Cussen. These are but a few names out of a long list.

There was one fact which so wide a Guild of Catholic writers brought home to us - the matter was raised at an early meeting by some member - the great inexhaustible number of important Catholic articles that could be written by members - but where in Ireland would a whole army of consistent writers find publication ? Here was the crux . The outlet as far as an Irish Catholic periodical press was concerned was altogether too limited. The lesson, indeed, that the Catholic Writers' Guild taught was that the future activities of such a Circle must be directed as far as the printed word is concerned to those larger fields that lie outside Ireland. And yet any international Press Guide will show you what much smaller states and countries than ours are able to do towards supporting a host of Catholic periodicals ! If it could be part of the programme of a future Guild or Circle to carry out through its country supporters an intensive system of organisation, good results would, I am sure, accrue.

Meanwhile, the late Father MacInerney, O.P. , the accomplished Dominican writer and Editor, who took a deep interest in the Guild, reminded me on one occasion that the Catholic writer who wished to express his views on the vital questions of the hour, or who had a social reform to advocate, seemed to overlook the great medium of publicity that lay daily at his disposal. He referred to the columns of our secular newspapers, which were always open to consider letters from readers. His point was that here was a weapon which we were not turning to our use.

On the social and cultural side of the Guild, many look back to that richly entertaining and literary evening at Jury's hotel, when T.C. Murray read one of his unpublished plays.

Our Society was indeed "news" when its guest at luncheon was Sir Philip Gibbs, the famous war correspondent. I can remember him with his keen ascetic profile, his silvering hair and his soldierly bearing as he chatted encouragingly with us. Out of what a world of tumult he had come - from the Balkan flames of 1912 to the truce of Amiens, when the war-mad nations at last had time to take toll of their harvesting and count their thirteen million dead! the election of Popes, the death-bed of kings, royal weddings, State intrigues, political upheavals - these were the settings, grim or glorious, in which Sir Philip Gibbs had lived and moved for more than a quarter of a century. But this unassuming man, conscious only of the responsibility of his great calling, spoke firmly and calmly of the Catholic writer and his power for good. "Ideas," he said, "are the force behind most movements which influence the minds of men and women. Provided the writer is mindful of his duties as a Christian, he can do much to counteract and modify the passions, hatreds and suspicions from the effects of which the world has already suffered so much."

The luncheon discussion had its lighter side. In the tributes that were being paid to Sir Philip Gibbs, the words, "great Fleet Street journalist," were used more than once. Colm O'Lochlainn, associating himself with the vote of thanks, rose with a cheerful twinkle: "And since I too work in Fleet Street ------"

Laughter ran round the crowded table when it was swiftly recollected that London's busy street of ink had a humble Dublin namesake ! And surely Colm O Lochlainn, of the Sign of the Three Candles, was privileged in making this delicious pun.

And now a glimpse of another Dublin literary evening: Compton Mackenzie with his cloak and his short trim beard - looking every inch a Scot - yet picturesque as a figure out of Elizabethan literature. He is talking about a new Irish novel and why he would give it a prize. Little Padraic Colum, vaguely Goldsmithian about his fine head and forehead, is now discussing the short story; a few minutes later and it is James Stephens saying why he gives an award for this poem or that. Lennox Robinson asks Lord Dunsany to come up for third prize for his play, but there is no Lord Dunsany to respond. Meanwhile in the class that looks on at this prize-giving there is goodly company, including the Aga Khan (whom you must not always associate with racing winners, for he is a writer too, and has written scathingly about the false decadent *credo* of Omar Khayyam). G.K.C. is the magnet of many eyes, while near him sits Augustus John, eminent English portrait painter. He himself somewhat resembles the portraits of Robert Louis Stevenson. But this is another literary Festival - it has grown up in connection with the first Aonach Tailteann.

When I met Padraic Colum I told him of our gratitude to him for the lines from "The Plougher":-

18

"O man, standing lone and bowed earthward,
Thy day is a task near its close;
give thanks to the night-giving God."

But Mr. Colum is modest about his art in prose and verse; yet I think a writer likes to hear that something which he has wrought well has not been dropped wholly neglected in the wilderness.

True, it was not always through the Literary Societies I met and came to know some of Dublin's well-known literary figures. I was introduced to Mr. Stephen Gwynn after a public dinner in an Irish provincial hotel. One thinks of a writer or poet sometimes, not by the entire bulk or volume of his output, but by a single fragment of beauty that has caught in the mind. It may be a stanza - a mere line. Thus, when Chesterton's name is mentioned, Don John of Austria comes to mind; somebody speaks of Yeats, and I think of the "Ballad of Peter Gilligan." I went to hear Mr. Desmond Fitzgerald, the last Minister for Defence, at a recent election meeting, not because of anything political he had to say; no; I wanted to see and hear the man who wrote "The Saint," that beautiful and moving play which was produced at the Abbey Theatre many years ago. Thus the stanza he had written far-off in the romance of boyhood, and which I now recalled to him, seemed to Mr. Gwynn like a wistful echo from a forgotten country:-

"For your sake I loved the columned forest,
Where the ways forever meet, forever part;
But I fear that I have lost my way forever
To the green and sunny glade that is your heart."

Death and distance have cast a shadow on the literary Dublin of even less than twenty years ago. Katharine Tynan - I look on my meeting with her as a memory that has something of a legendary quality. She was in the evening of her days then, but with all that charm of personality that never grows old. Sympathetic and encouraging and with a kindly candour, I must have been the last in a long list of literary beginners to be privileged with her judgement of the lyric line. And whether she spoke of one's verse or recalled at your request her London literary friendships of the nineties, one glimpsed in the flash of her glance a certain spiritual joy. One could truly endorse what "AE" wrote of her: "Katharine Tynan says of herself (in one of her poems): 'I was born under a kind star.' It is true. She is happy in religion, friendship, children, instantly kindling at any beauty in garden flowers, in sky and clouds. She has, too, that spiritual bravery which makes beauty out of death or sorrow. A friend passes, and he is sped on his journey, not with despair, but with hope, almost with imaginative gaiety." And when I recall her ideal poet's home near Blackrock, with its secluded walk, its giant trees, and its garden overhanging with blossom, I seem to see in vision all the ideal homes in which she lived and her happy, crowded life full of friendship and travel. And what friends - Patmore, Alice Meynell, Lionel Johnson, and the author of "The Hound of Heaven." When I asked her about Alice Meynell she was touched, and there was lyrical pathos in her voice as she recreated for me that beloved figure of the higher Muse - her ethereal quality suggesting a flower out of immortal fields blooming amid our earthly wind and soil. But here I am wandering from the literary clubs to the poet-homes of Dublin, and that is a chapter for another day.

Tara - Its Significance for One Visitor

When I lived in Dublin some years ago almost every St. Patrick's Day found me spending an hour on the Hill of Tara. There was more than one reason why I visited Tara so frequently. It called to me - as it calls to me still - because of its royal history; because of its association with the dawn of Christianity - and there is a third and very human reason for my visits to Tara. Standing on the pastoral upland, provided the visibility was favourable, I could see twenty-five or thirty miles away on the North-west horizon the hill above my home !..

Twenty years ago in the shadow of that childhood hill I thinned the turnips in my father's fields, and saw far off on the plains of Meath, the horizon that was Tara. It was over this horizon the morning broke....

The most pleasant of my visits to Tara, however, took place last July. It was a clear summer day free from mists and hazes, and Loughcrew, the Ben-of-Fore, and all those hills on the distant circle of the horizon were clearly visible. There were sleek bullocks browsing in the royal grass beside me, for if one excepts the wind-worn statue of St. Patrick and the unpretentious stone pillar, Tara is grass. Nevertheless, I felt as I looked down on the great plain of Meath on that summer evening that the kings of old in choosing Tara had chosen well. Like all upland places it is exhilarating. The stranger coming on Tara unaware could not imagine that this green hill had been the subject of mighty and learned books; that it had engaged the attention of the foremost European scholars and antiquarians; that those mounds and ramparts and ridges of green earth had given rise to so much scholastic theory and vain conjecture. And it will probably always be so about Tara. Who will say the last word ?

As for me I am satisfied with the fundamentals, that is that Tara had a royal and pagan significance, and that it was on this green height Paganism and Christianity met in one moment of tremendous drama. Patrick had all the qualifications of the

21

successful ambassador, and he had the courage of a great soldier, hence the events of Ireland's first Holy Saturday.

Those events are all familiar history - the mandate of King Laoghaire regarding his birthday fire on Tara.

"No fire may be lit upon hill or hearth
Till the King's strong fire in his kingly mirth
Leaps upward from Tara's palace steeps !"

"Yet Patrick has lighted his paschal fire
At Slane.......;"

The summons of the King, the meeting of Laoghaire and our National Apostle - all I repeat are familiar history; but when are such events to be raised above the plane of history into the realms of living and memorable drama ?

What history-book could depict Patrick's meetings with Laoghaire as poetry can depict it ? And this brings me to my chief affection for Tara.

When I think of the historic hill to-day, I do not trouble to reconstruct for myself the old old picture that is beyond history's ken; the Tara of the kings that reigned before Laoghaire nor yet the festive board scene with its "chiefs and ladies bright," its harpers and its jesters; nor am I so much concerned with the Tara of the Druids and legislators and its importance as ancient Erin's Court of Appeal.

Thinking of Tara I do not consult aerial photographs or maps indicating every square foot of the hill, but I linger over the Tara that first Easter Sunday morning in Erin, not as the historian describes it, but as it emerges from the poet's pen of Aubrey de Vere:

Patrick is on his way to Tara in response to Laoghaire's summons, and though the morning is charged with mystery and suspense and cataclysmal possibilities yet what a peaceful picture this is:

Then forth to Tara he fared full lowly;
The Staff of Jesus was in his hand;
Eight priests paced after him, chanting slowly
Printing their steps on the dewy land.
It was the Resurrection morn;
The lark sang loud o'er the springing corn;
The dove was heard and the hunter's horn.

That is the picture - the dewy lyrical morning of the poet that I love to recall when I remember Tara.

The peace and beauty of that scene was but a prelude to the tranquillity and success that marked Patrick's mission throughout Ireland. There were no spears drawn in opposition; there was no bloodshed.

And recalling that lyrical morning I look north-west at one dark hill amongst the hills that form an un-even horizon. And I know that it is the Ben-of-Fore. Beneath it I plucked shamrocks on more care-free mornings than these - beneath it, too, above the music of cascaded waters lies the grave of her who pinned the first shamrock in my school-child's cap. There, too, is the National School where first I learned Aubrey de Vere's poem on "St. Patrick and the Bard," which has so endeared Tara to me.

Ireland - Her Landscape and Her People
Foreign Impressions of Past Centuries

From the days of Giraldus Cambrensis down to G.K. Chesterton, visitors from other countries have toured our island leaving to us afterwards interesting records and impressions of their sojourn amongst us. Sometimes there were English visitors who came here with deep-rooted prejudices and, perhaps, a little timidity, only to find that their pre-conceived notions were all wrong and that their visit to Ireland became afterwards one of the very pleasant memories of their lives.

Famous Tourists of the Past

There was scarcely a literary man of note in the England of the nineteenth century who did not pay us a visit. Wordsworth has left on record his unstinted praise of Killarney; Thackeray declared that he would travel a hundred miles alone to look down from Croagh Patrick on the waters of Clew Bay and incidentally, he pays this compliment to Limerick. "I never met a greater number of kind, pleasing, clever-looking faces among any set of people." Alfred Austin, an English Poet-Laureate of a later date wrote: "I went to Ireland in search of natural beauty and human kindness, and nowhere have I met more of either." Again, the English eighteenth century traveller, Arthur Young, observed: "May we not recognise in this the hand of bounteous Providence, which has given perhaps the most stony soil in Europe the moistest climate...... But the rocks here are covered with verdure; those of limestone, with only a thin covering of mould, have the softest and most beautiful turf imaginable."

A Tribute to Kilkenny

Mrs. Felicia Hemans, the Liverpool born poetess who died just one hundred years ago and who achieved considerable fame in her time, came to visit Ireland in her last years. She had spent periods at the famous places of beauty in England. Scotland and Wales, including the celebrated Lake District, yet this is what she writes of Woodstock in Co. Kilkenny. "The scenery of this place is magnificent; of a style which I think I prefer to every other; wild profound glens rich with every hue and form of foliage, and a rapid river sweeping through them, now lost, and now lighting up the deep woods with sudden flashes of its waves."

A French Visitor in the Eighteenth Century

Of unusual interest also is a set of Mss. in the National Library of Paris. They are the diaries or notebooks as yet unpublished of a French traveller in Ireland in the eighteenth century. The diarist was Baron Charles Coquebert de Montbret, who was French Consul in Dublin (1790-1793.) He notes with genuine pity the poverty and hardships of the poor both in country and city. An odd document amongst these papers is a bill for dinner served to him on board a boat on the Grand Canal. He was travelling from Dublin to Monasterevan. Travel by these inland waterways was then very popular. One secured bed and breakfast for the modest sum of eightpence. In journeying through the country our French traveller also noticed that outside many cottages a white rag or cloth flew flag-wise from a tiny pole. He soon learned this indicated that milk was for sale within, and he immediately treated himself to a glass.

Ireland's Devotion to the Rosary

In the reign of King James 11, another French visitor who was travelling through an Irish countryside ravished by Cromwell some forty years before, comments on the intense devotion of the Irish people to the Rosary. It was not unusual to find a person "sitting behind a bush in ye field saying over the beads or Rosary with great devotion and earnestness."

In the more recent Irish past of seventy years ago, Sir John Forbes, physician to Queen Victoria, published a "Memorandum of his tour in Ireland," and in it he noted also the widespread devotion to the Blessed Virgin.

Visitors in Spirit

On the Ireland of the Golden Age we have had in the past as in the present many foreign commentators. They were writers who had visited us as it were in spirit. Other continental writers and scholars have studied deeply that greater Ireland of Faith and learning represented by our wandering missionaries in every European country. Thus in a spiritual sense, writers like Montalembert and Zimmer were our visitors, for if they did not come to our shores they became intimate with our earlier outposts - centres like Gaul and Bobbio.

Even when Doctor Johnson in his tour of the Hebrides and the Scottish isles visited Iona and paid his famous tribute to the Island of Colmcille in the light of its hallowed remains, he was paying a tribute to Ireland of the Saints.

Oh! To be in Ireland .... Now that April's here!

To be in Ireland in April!....

An exile in time and distance it was always in the last month of the spring that the memory-picture emerged sharp and clear.   Now and then in the breathing spaces of a busy existence he recalled it. Then the factories and warehouses, the alien streets and masonry became less tangible than the visionary greenery of the April hedges of Ireland.   And so he would set out on this little walk of the mind, forgetting the seas of distance and the years of exile.

He would start at the edge of the bog and at the flat wet stones where the cows drank he would stay a long, long while.   The insect life of the marshy air; the tremulous minnows in the still water.   And that distant islet of tufted sedge where the wild duck must surely have built a nest.   Large and warm those blue-green eggs in the rushy nest on the bank. What a discovery! Not a wild fowl's after all - but Bessy Mangan's lame duck - always a rover - had been laying out.   "God lave you yer eyesight", said Bessie when she heard the news.

And now the wooden stile - old, makeshift, but firm - half hidden in a tangle of briar and whitethorn.   This way he must go if he would follow the boundary ditch towards the hill.

Yet it was with a little heart-heaviness he turned his face from the bog.   There, somehow, were his real roots and not in the wind-parched uplands.   Out of the bog-garden's green sallies his cradle had been made, and it was the warm summer fragrances of wild honey and moss that first blew in over the half door of childhood.

But the long fields over the boundary fence of his father's land were fresh and sweet with the young sounds of Spring.   The pet lambs careering wildly towards the farmyard gate in answer to a mealtime call.   Above the pine plantation and higher still over the rocks the morning was lyrical - the lark was everywhere today and the whole blue sky was shining and singing.

The old man quietly pursued his stroll of memory; the long stems of the furze bushes - he never remembered having seen them shorter and the bushes seemed never to have grown older. But now surely they were young again with the Spring - and laden with yellow silken blossom. In a sunny sheltered clearing by the hedge the massed primroses - they could have been the very same flowers of other years - the same primroses frail and immortal.

Slowly, carefully, through a paling of rusty wire and into the next field. At length in his long-loved grassy walk of memory the old man came to the topmost pasture. Here the shamrocks grew in abundance. He remembered the first prayers his mother taught him, and he saw the shamrocks again through a mist. He looked up - that whole horizon line was engraved on his memory forever - this hill, that rise of ground - the blue-dim woods in the April distance. He was going downwards again; he stopped to take up a bush that the wind had blown out of a gap; he fixed it securely in its place. Field after field - slowly, slowly. The April grass again in his own fields and the sun shining! What nourishment this for a home-starved heart!

The thatch of the long farmhouse showed through the trees. And now he was back again on the boreen by the bog. The bog .... so his stroll of memory was drawing to an end. The sun shone clear through the bog stream showing the white gravel at its bottom. The budding marigolds, branched downwards to the water. But the white land of daisies dreaming in sun - the picture was growing faint, the exile-reality was returning. Ah! to be in Ireland in April!

Exiles of Ireland - St. Patrick's Day Reflections

From the far places of their exile they remember her today - the Ireland of their spring-time, the land of morning. As the sun suddenly looks out on a window of blue amongst the massed clouds, so each exile has his Patrick's Day vision when the mists of time and of distance seem to have fallen apart and the ancestral rocks and hills emerge again as of old amid the moods and changes of an Irish March day.

What do they remember? Who knows? Parent and school-mate - tree and briary gap - the detailed features of hedge and moor - the colour of the turf smoke - the sunlight beaming over the half door.

When we contemplate the exiled children of the Gael scattered to the four winds, many thoughts sad and joyful come to mind. How many of them are valued as mere robots - cogs in the wheels of some gigantic machinery in mine or factory where everything is alien and godless - where wealth is the supreme aim and the priceless ideals of Catholic youth are lost to all nurturing or fostering environment? We have learned much of late of the pitfalls of disaster that await the unwary feet of the Irish emigrant, and we look forward to the day when the resources of our own land will provide a comfortable living at home for every son and daughter of Ireland.

Meanwhile it is on St. Patrick's Day that our far-scattered island family whom the seven seas divide and sub-divide are one in spirit.

On St. Patrick's Day, we think, perhaps, of the emigrant who went from us and who could have stayed, but the thirst for wandering and adventure in strange places would be satisfied. We think of those who have succeeded as the world spells success, but who in the intoxication of their fame and riches have, we fear, broken all links with their native earth in losing the Faith of their fathers.

But what of the Irish exiles of the Higher Adventure, of the Field Afar? Do we remember them on St. Patrick's Day, not merely individually but collectively? They have gone forth to build no earthly city, but to advance the spiritual empire of St. Patrick to the loneliest outposts of the world. Their empire is unfrontiered by tropical palms or arctic snows, and if we may be allowed the metaphor, their great dream is to rekindle the Easter Fire of Slane Hill on every height from Fujiyama to the Rockies.

Those missionaries of Ireland - her priests and nuns and brothers who are in the direct tradition of the Golden Age of Columbanus, have gone into voluntary exile. Peregrinari pro Christo is their motto - to be exiled for Christ. Thus their exile differs from that of all others, and it was their choice to part with home and kindred and all human ties of childhood and youth to bear the message of Patrick into every land. Their deeds unchronicled and unsung, those Irish pioneers of the gospel beyond the reach of the world's limelight, oftentimes pursue alone their missionary endeavour, their heroic conquests. If their efforts and triumphs were judged by temporal or earthly standards they would have many times over won the laurels of a Caesar or Alexander.

And when remembering our exiles on St. Patrick's Day, there should be a special prayerful remembrance of our missionary exiles. Think not that their human minds have forgotten the March mists on our morning hills, the brown horizon of the bog, the dew on the green roadsides of home. To them as to all exiles, especially on this our National Festival, the touching stanzas apply:

> *"I think if I lay dying in some land*
> *Where Ireland is no more than just a name*
> *My soul would travel back to find that strand*
> *From whence it came.*
>
> *And then the Angelus,*
> *I'd surely see the swaying bell against a golden sky*
> *So God, who kept the love of home in me*
> *Would let me die".*

Francis Ledwidge and 1916. A note on "The Blackbirds"

Just twenty-one years ago a beautiful poem was written by an Irish poet and some day it will be taken from the book in which it originally appeared and set down perhaps in one anthology after another and few if any will guess its significance. Its title is "The Blackbirds" and to the casual reader it may mean no more than a lament for the birds that some callous fowler has shot. It will recall perhaps verses of lesser merit by T.D. Sullivan, when he called upon the sportsman, "to turn his guns away and spare the little singing birds that sing upon the spray". But if this little poem "The Blackbirds" was written by a poet-soldier in the uniform of England he was an Irishman thinking and feeling over the tragedy of his Irish brother poets - the "Blackbirds" he calls them because of the sweetness of their song - Pearse, MacDonagh and Plunkett. The author of "The Blackbirds" was Francis Ledwidge - the truest singer that the fields of Ireland have ever inspired. As I have already the courteous and unreserved permission of Lord Dunsany - Ledwidge's literary executor - to quote from the poet I have no hesitation now in giving here "The Blackbirds" in its entirety.

I heard the Poor Old Woman say
"At break of day the fowler came
And took my blackbirds from their songs
Who loved me well thro' shame and blame.

No more from lovely distances
Their songs shall bless me mile by mile
Nor to white Ashbourne call me down
To wear my crown another while.

With bended flowers the angels mark
For the skylark the place they lie
From there its little family
Shall dip their wings first in the sky.

And when the first surprise of flight
Sweet songs excite, from the far dawn
Shall there come blackbirds loud with love
Sweet echoes of the singers gone.

But in the lonely hush of eve
Weeping I grieve the silent bills"
I heard the Poor Old Woman say
In Derry of the little hills.

When Ledwidge wrote this poem in the summer of 1916 he was stationed, I think, at the British military headquarters in Londonderry. Hence "Derry of the little hills". Though I often thought that he was actually home on holiday in Meath when he wrote it and that there could easily be such an obscure townland named "Derry" in the neighbourhood of his own Boyneside country. However, if the poem ever appears as an isolated piece in an anthology or representative collection of Irish poetry it will need to be explained in some sort of brief footnote. Otherwise its significance and much of its beauty will be lost.

When Francis Ledwidge wrote from France to Katherine Tynan - I have a copy of his letter before me - in July, 1917, the very month in which he was killed he has this touching statement: "If I survive the war I have great hopes of writing something that will live. If not, I trust to be remembered in my own land for one or two things which its long sorrow inspired". What were those one or two things? Of the five or six poems by Ledwidge which Easter, 1916, inspired, "The Blackbirds" to my mind is the best. Other readers may favour "Thomas MacDonagh" which is becoming better known with the passing of the years:

"He shall not hear the bittern cry
In the wild sky, where he is lain
Nor voices of the sweeter birds
Above the wailing of the rain.

Nor shall he know when loud March blows
Thro' slanting snows her fanfare shrill
Blowing to flame the golden cup
Of many an upset daffodil.

But when the Dark Cow leaves the moor
And pastures poor with greedy weeds

Perhaps he'll hear her low at morn
Lifting her horn in pleasant meeds".

His poem "Thro' Bogac Ban" where he met the Silent Wandering Man is also of the same inspiration and did he not mention Joseph Plunkett's name the verses here again would be without historic significance - though beauty would remain. And in another poem in this group - though he is far away amid the World War himself - he has heard the distant echoes of resurgent Ireland.

"Her chains are falling with a chime
Sweet as bells in Heaven town".

but hard on this has come the news of the Maxwell executions:

"But, harpers, leave your harps aside,
And, poets, leave awhile your dreams,
The storm has come upon the tide
And Cathleen weeps among her streams".

There is another poem which he wrote in September or October, 1916. It is called "Ireland" and could well be singled out as Ledwidge's Apologia. Here he tells his own story in relation to the Irish Rising - making his attitude clear in the last stanza. It must be set down in full:

"I called you by sweet names by wood and linn
You answered not because my voice was new
And you were listening for the hounds of Finn
and the long hosts of Lugh.

And so, I came unto a windy height
And cried my sorrow, but you heard no wind
For you where listening to small ships in flight
And the wail on hills behind.

And then I left you, wandering the War
Armed with will, from distant goal to goal
To find you at the last free as of yore
Or die to save your soul.

And then you called to us from far and near
To bring your crown from out the deeps of time
It is my grief your voice I couldn't hear
In such a distant clime".

That last stanza establishes Ledwidge's ideals as one with those of the poet-leaders at home in Dublin. Surely he has touched greatness in that line: "To bring your crown from out the deeps of time".

Lastly in a poem of delicate faery and childish fancy he links his own name with those of Pearse and Plunkett.

The title of the verses is "At Currabee". He tells us of the fairies at this homeland place of grass and hawthorn. There are hard at work every night mending their little boots; the material they use is tough - the wings of bats. And they sing and their song is of a free Ireland.

"So I heard Joseph Plunkett say
You know he heard them but last May
And when the night is very cold
They warm their hands against the light
Of stars that make the waters gold
Where they are labouring all the night
So Pearse said, and he knew the truth
Among the stars he spent his youth".

And though pledged to fight on a far foreign field Ledwidge fain would have his memory and ideals one with those of Pearse and Plunkett for the concluding stanza of the same poem runs:

"And, I myself, have often heard
Their singing as the stars went by
For am I not of those who reared
The banner of old Ireland high
From Dublin town to Turkey's shores
And where the Vardar loudly roars?"

Out of these poems and out of all that Ledwidge has written he would ask us to remember him in "one or two poems" which the long sorrows of Ireland inspired. I venture to suggest for the first time that the two poems he had in mind were "The Blackbirds" and "Ireland". Look back and read them over again and say if in part at least they are not two of the loveliest lyrics which Easter 1916 inspired - indeed two of the loveliest lyrics in Anglo-Irish poetry.

Our Lady of Ireland

There is a big book coming from the pen of a gifted Irish scholar and writer, Dr. Helena Concannon, M.A., and when it arrives we trust, in fact we feel certain, that it will do full justice to a subject that has long been neglected. It is the claim of the Blessed Virgin to be called in a very special way "Queen of Ireland". "All generations shall call me blessed." In those quiet Judean hills when her whole soul became absorbed in the Magnificat and she foretold that all generations should call her blessed, is it more than fancy to suggest that she had in mind some countries where this prophecy would be fulfilled in the face of fierce and terrible opposition. Nowhere were the words "all generations shall call me blessed" more strongly challenged with fire and sword than in Ireland.

Gaelic literature from the earliest days of Christianity in Ireland and Irish history itself supply ample evidence of Erin's devotion to the Mother of God. We recall how the name was distinguished from that of all other Marys by the use of Muire. Otherwise the name was Maire. "It is not without purpose," Dr. Concannon has already written "that out of the jewel case of Mary's shining titles the ' golden treasury of her praises' our Irish forefathers chose as the name above all other names by which they loved to address her, the title of 'Mother of God'. Its choice was a deliberate protest against certain heresies; and its use from the earliest times is a striking proof of Irish orthodoxy."

"No less striking" she goes on "is the zeal testified against those heretics who would deny Our Lady's perpetual virginity. 'The One Son of Mary' is an expression even yet very common on the lips of Irish speakers - and when they use it they are claiming, unconsciously, their part in a great tradition - taking their place in a mighty succession of Irish champions of "Blessed Mary ever Virgin" extending over the centuries to the days of St. Mochta of Louth, whose 'profession of Faith' expressing belief in the doctrine, is said to have been presented to Pope St. Leo the Great about AD 460.

Everywhere in the documents and records that exist regarding the Golden Age we find evidence of the same devotion amongst the Irish Saints. Beautiful poems and tributes to our Blessed Lady written by Irish saints have survived all the centuries. Notable amongst them is a lovely prayer composed by Brendan the Navigator.

Dr. Concannon also reminds us of the early tributes in art and sculpture which our people paid to the Blessed Virgin. She refers us to the Book of Kells itself, that masterpiece amongst our illuminated MSS, where there is a picture of the Blessed Virgin and her Child, "her head surrounded by a glory ornamented with three crosses."

Throughout all the subsequent centuries, despite vandalism, and right down to the Elizabethan persecution, some of the shrines of Mary in Ireland became famous centres of pilgrimage and devotion. Amongst the most notable was the Shrine of Our Lady of Trim (Co. Meath). Here again the origin of the statue of Our Lady of Trim is traceable to St. Patrick's time, or to be more correct to that of Loman - Patrick's nephew. Loman was the first bishop consecrated in Ireland. In mediaeval times the fame of the shrine of Our Lady of Trim spread not only to the four corners of Ireland but overseas. Everywhere in the ancient records we find abundant reference to this shrine. In the annals of the Four Masters especially we find notable entries concerning "Our Lady of Trim". Thither again and again came rich and poor, Gael and Saxon, soldier and scholar, members of royal households - all united in a Marian pilgrimage.

But the fame of Our Lady of Trim which grew with the centuries suffered at last a sacrilegious eclipse. Let the Four Masters in their necessarily brief manner tell the story -

"AD 1537. A heresy and a new error sprang up in England through pride, vain glory, avarice and lust, so that the men of England went into opposition to the Pope and Rome. They broke down the monasteries and sold their roofs and bells. They afterwards burned the images, shrines and relics of the saints of Ireland and England; they likewise burned the celebrated image of

37

the Blessed Virgin Mary at Trim which used to perform miracles and wonders, which used to heal the blind, the deaf and the cripples, and the persons affected with all kinds of diseases."

Other centres of Marian pilgrimage in those far off days in Ireland were the Shrine of Our Lady of Navan, Our Lady of Coleraine, Our Lady of Limerick, Our Lady of Youghal and our Lady of Galway. The three last mentioned images of Our Lady which happily are still preserved, are inseparably associated with the story of the Dominican Fathers in Ireland. The Fathers of the Rosary, despite persecution and exile and all the horrors of the Penal days, were untiring in their efforts to spread devotion to Our Blessed Lady. So that if famous shrines like that of Trim have been reduced to ashes centuries ago, the visitor may still see the Youghal statue of Our Lady of Graces. It is enshrined in St. Mary's, Cork, while our Lady of Galway has found a new pedestal in the Dominican church on the outskirts of the Claddagh, and our Lady of Limerick may be seen in St. Saviour's in that city.

Dr. Concannon in her forthcoming book will also have a good deal to tell about statues and shrines of Our Lady associated with the early days of the Jesuits in Ireland.

A great chapter could certainly be written on the subject of the Blessed Virgin in Irish literature. Readers of the Irish Rosary are, however, familiar with the scholarly work of a contributor on this vast subject. However, I take the liberty of quoting in full "The Keening of Mary" as translated by Padraic Pearse. It is a poignantly lovely thing.

"O Peter, O Apostle has thou seen my bright love?
(M'Óchón agus m'óchón Ó!)
I saw Him even now in the midst of His foemen".
(M'Óchón agus m'óchón Ó!)

Come hither, two Marys, till ye keen my bright love
(M'Óchón agus m'óchón Ó!)
What have we to keen unless we keen His bones?
(M'Óchón agus m'óchón Ó!)

Who is that stately man on the tree of passion?
(M'Óchón agus m'óchón Ó!)
Dost thou not know thy Son, O Mother?
(M'Óchón agus m'óchón Ó!)

And is that the little Son I carried nine months?
(M'Óchón agus m'óchón Ó!)
And is that the little Son that was born in the stable?
(M'Óchón agus m'óchón Ó!)

And is that the little Son that was nursed on Mary's breast?
(M'Óchón agus m'ochón Ó!)
Hush, O Mother, and be not sorrowful!
(M'Óchón agus m'óchón Ó!)

And is that the hammer that struck home the nails through Thee?
(M'Óchón agus m'óchón Ó!)
And is that the spear that went through Thy white side?
(M'Óchón agus m'óchón Ó!)

And is that the crown of thorns that crowned Thy beauteous head?
(M'Óchón agus m'óchón Ó!)
Hush, O Mother, and be not sorrowful!
(M'Óchón agus m'óchón Ó!)

Hush, O Mother and be not sorrowful!
(M'Óchón agus m'óchón Ó!)
The women of My keening are yet unborn, little Mother
(M'Óchón agus m'óchón Ó!)

O woman who weepest, by this My death
(M'Óchón agus m'óchón Ó!)
There will be hundreds today in the garden of Paradise
(M'Óchón agus m'óchón Ó!)

Beneath the poem, Pearse added this note: "I heard 'The Keening of Mary' from a woman of Moycullen, in Iar Connacht. Her own name was Mary Clancy, and she was married, as she told me, to one of the Keadys. I have heard nothing more exquisite than her low sobbing recitative, instinct with a profoundly felt emotion. There was a great horror in her voice at 'S an é sin an casúr' ('And is that the hammer, etc.) and with the next stanza the chant rose into a wail. She cried pitifully and struck her breast several times during the recitation. It is a very precious thing for the world that in the homes of Ireland there are still men and women who can shed tears for the sorrows of Mary and her Son."

And thus everywhere in the old poetry of the Gael we find references to the "white-footed, deathless, inviolate, bright bodied maiden" that was Mary.

The story of the Rosary in Ireland and the story of the heroism and self-sacrifice of the Irish Dominicans - the Fathers of the Rosary as they were called - these in themselves make histories of our country that are glorious and inspiring.

Many famous travellers, and indeed unknown but observant visitors who have come amongst us in past centuries, have left on record vivid impressions of Ireland's devotion to the Rosary. Now it is a French visitor, in the reign of King James II, again it is the Protestant Sir John Forbes, physician to Queen Victoria. Note the former's observation after travelling through a countryside ravished by Cromwell. It was not unusual to find a person "sitting behind a bush in ye field saying over the beads or Rosary with great devotion and earnestness."

In our own day some of the sweetest sounds of the Irish countryside and indeed of the town and city tell of Mary. For, three times a day the Angelus Bell in the distant tower rings over houses and valleys and woods and again in the hush of evening that sweetest sound of Irish twilights - the voice of the Rosary recited by the hearth of home comes to the ear of the passer-by. In one voice also through the countless branches of Sodalities and Confraternities the heart of Ireland goes forth in prayer and hymn to Mary.

Coming down to modern times also one could safely say that there is no Irish Catholic poet of note who has not yet sung of Mary.

40

This is only in keeping with the tradition of our ancient and mediaeval poets. Padraic Colum's "O men from the fields" (a lullaby that truly makes earth and heaven one) has found a worthy place in John McCormack's repertoire and has gone into many anthologies both in these countries and abroad :

" Mavourneen is going
From me and from you
Where Mary will fold her
In mantle of blue".

It was a non-Catholic Irish poet of today who saw the "sky above Tibradden as blue as Mary's cloak" and the same singer who enshrined in a haunting lyric another echo of Mary - the swaying Angelus Bell seen against a golden evening sky.   Katherine Tynan, Teresa Brayton, Cathal O'Byrne, - Daniel Corkery in his play "The Yellow Bittern", Francis Ledgwidge - The Lily of Israel - the Mother of all mothers has inspired all.

Listen how Seamus MacManus tells of the death of that sweet poetess, Ethna Carbery ....."On a beautiful morn of the glorious Eastertide her task was done; she only paused to cast back one last look; and then still telling through her tightening fingers the brown beads that cheered her on her way, she stepped over the crest and went out of sight forever".   Aye the brown beads that cheered her on her way.   It was the brown beads too that cheered Ireland along the perilous way of the Penal years.   It was the beads also that cheered and encouraged children of Ireland no less great than O'Connell himself, who always turned to Mary in the critical moments of his public life.

In our art and song; in our legend and tradition; in our history and in our literature through the whole fabric of the daily life of our people the name of Mary is entertained.

Well indeed may we call her Our Lady of Ireland - the immortal Queen of our country.

Ireland's Ambassadors of the Pen

I must be pardoned, if at the outset I quote substantially something I wrote long before this discussion was initiated. I take any European scholar, let him be German, Italian, Swiss, French or Belgian; he realises of course that the foundations upon which the centuries-old culture and civilisation of his own country rest, are largely the work of the early Irish monks. Now he wishes to learn something of the contemporary life of that land of poet - saints to which his own country is so hugely indebted. Are not the missionary names of early Ireland preserved in the streets and squares of his own town. Are not these names that bespeak holiness and learning enshrined in village and canton; in islands on the Rhine; aye, in the very mountains from whose summits you may look at Rome.

Thinking of that land that in its golden age had been a light to Europe from the Hebrides to the Appenines, may not our European scholar ask what is the life, the spirit of that great land today. Where is he to find it mirrored? Why of course in its literature. And with his mind fired with the epic deeds of Columbanus and the exile poetry of Columcille he goes to a library to seek for the soul of twentieth century Ireland.

Let us say that he goes to the National Library of his own land whether it be in Berlin or Paris, Brussels or even in London. He asks for some of the representative names of contemporary Ireland in poetry, fiction, and the drama: of course, why not, - it will be the old familiar list. Yeats, AE, Liam O'Flaherty, James Stephens. He opens AE's poems. Can this be the representative poetic mouthpiece of Ireland - these vague theosophic wanderings, these queer theories of birth and rebirth. Is this the type of poetry that in the twentieth century represents Ireland throughout the world - Ireland with its centuries-old Catholic tradition?

The so-called Irish Literary Renaissance of the beginning of this century has produced poetry by "representative" Irish poets that would represent or interpret us sure enough if instead of the symbol of the Cross - Indian temples or Chinese pagoda rose above our hills and villages. Why it was only the other day one of those poets of the "Irish Renaissance" now resident in the East actually embraced Hinduism. Here is an admission by the late AE (he was writing of a truly representative Irish poet, Katherine Tynan).

"Katherine Tynan", he wrote, "was the earliest singer in that awakening of our imagination which has been spoken of as the Irish Renaissance. I think she had as much natural sunlight in her as the movement ever attained. (That is certainly true. M.W.) "The Irish imagination" AE goes on "is little interested in normal humanity and its affections. It deserts centres for circumferences. It goes adventuring in Overworld, in fairy, in fantasy, in Underworld, in the crypts and sewers of the soul". He is thinking of course of the "Irish imagination" out of which the Academy of Letters has largely developed.

In other words, this imagination AE has in mind wanders everywhere except to the heart of the Catholic life of our people which is reflected in the normal day-to-day life in Ireland.

Now to return to the bewildered foreign scholar seeking for the real Ireland through the big names in her literature.

Instead of the "gentle Ireland" in which the Faith is so tremendous an influence that its impress, its inward glow must illumine all our literature if it is to be representative, the stranger will find himself reading a page of human depravity; listening to the mouthings of one who has become a hero amongst his people because he has killed his father with a spade! Blasphemy, suicide, adultery? Insula sanctorum et doctorum, hast thou come to this?

The foreign scholar walks away from the library a sadly disillusioned man.

It will be seen at once that Ireland's ambassadors of the pen - those who would interpret for the world the life and spirit of this Catholic land - must be made known internationally through a system of co-operation and publicity. That is if their collective ambassadorship is to bear full fruit. What we look for today more than anything else is a great narrative poet-philosopher (but first of all a poet of the Faith) whose great lyric moments will encircle the globe as did the poetry of Yeats and AE. Just as the stiring ballad can breathe life into the dead bones of history, so poetry and poetry alone can become at once a just mirror and the highest form of literary expression.   I think now of those lines in Padraic Colum's "The Plougher";-

> "*O man standing lone and bowed earthward*
> *Your task is a day near its close*
> *Give thanks to the night-giving God*".

This is Irish earth and Irish Faith firmly and truly drawn - an Irish Millet painting "The Angelus". They are finished lines from the hand of a poet-artist. It is the voice of the poet-ambassador that ultimately reaches the farthest and endures the longest.   And Colum in this sense is an ambassador of whom we may be proud. But the great poet who will interpret us in a big body of work, is yet to come.

Meanwhile, the lyric quality which is the mark of true artistry distinguished the prose of nearly all the Catholic writers that have been named in this discussion.   But P.J. O'Connor Duffy who has already won international honours as a short story writer of our soil must not be forgotten.   Neither must Dr. Helena Concannon whose life of St. Columbanus America has already honoured. She has artistry of words as well as depth of scholarship.

Let this discussion on our ambassadors of the pen be a preliminary to action.   Let us analyse and examine and be certain of who they are.   Then when we have decided upon the names, let us devise a method of shouting those names from the housetops - and continue to shout them until the world hears.

"St. Paul would be a Journalist"

One of the healthy signs of the present time is the states recognition of the journalist and his calling. It was gladdening and encouraging to have the Papal Nuncio and the Ministers of State attend the recent Journalists' Dinner in Dublin.

Indeed I had often wondered if amid the tumult and the shouting of the past twenty years both in this country and in Europe generally the power of journalism for good or ill had ever been justly appreciated - or more important still - the mission of the journalist. It will be recalled that in the past Bishop Kettler made, what to the uninitiated must have sounded a startling declaration, "If St. Paul were with us today he would be a journalist".

It is just ten years ago that I was present at a luncheon at which Sir Philip Gibbs was the guest. Clearly I remember his utterance. Journalists and writers are the most important people in the world. This was the substance of his statement. "Ideas", he said "are the force behind most movements which influence the minds of men and women. Provided the writer is mindful of his duties as a Christian, he can do much to counteract and modify the passions, hatreds, and suspicions, from the effects of which the world has already suffered so much". But most striking of all are the words of the late Pope Pius X: "There is no nobler mission in the world today than that of the journalist. I bless the symbol of your office. My predecessors used to consecrate the swords and armour of Christian warriors. I am happy to draw down blessings on the pen of a Christian journalist".

The journalist or editor or contributor to the press does not himself know the limits of his influence. It is the newspaper that makes or unmakes the world's events in the public mind - that shapes national and international opinion.

Take for example the last Great War. What a meaningless and unknown muddle it would all have been (not indeed viewing it in retrospect it has been anything else), had we not the daily

45

journalistic records of the world's press to enable us to follow every attack and skirmish on the field.

It is, perhaps, at the war fronts of the world that the journalist's greatest responsibility lies. It is in the chronicler's veracity or otherwise that the attitude of the outside nations may be determined. But in the affairs of peace also the temper of the journalists' pen may kindle to enthusiasm or leave cold his great unknown public. And whether it be a civil war, like that in Spain, or the circumstances associated with the abdication of a king, it is the journalist who "creates" the event or the sensation for the public. Were it not for him the event as far as the average man is concerned non est. There has been no abdication; there is no civil war. So also with our great men - our statesmen, our militarists, our leaders, our dictators. Do we not in a sense "create" them as such - award them on their pedestals, or leave them in obscurity according to the measure of publicity we give them?

One could give many examples of the revolutionizing power of journalism and the victories it can achieve when it takes a great cause to its heart. I have in mind now an Irish editor who died some years ago. He founded an Irish-Ireland journal some forty years back and week after week through all those decades his pen was ceaseless in its pleading for a self-respecting, self-supporting nation. It waged an unrelenting war on the subservience the apeing and the sham - the West Britainism that was running like a spurious thread through our Gaelic fabric. He pleaded year in and year out for the products of our own hands, and our own soil - not to speak of our cultural self-expression, our language, our music, our literature. And if we are waking up at last, how much do we not owe to the pioneering of such editors and journals.

Yes, it is encouraging to realise that the work of the journalist is beginning to be appreciated at its just value. Besides representation on the Councils of the State, journalism must soon find its place also on the programme of our schools and universities. Training in Catholic journalism has long since been an important feature in the colleges and universities of America.

In a Catholic country like ours, it is but fitting that the ethics of journalism, the pen in its relation to Christian principles and other such vital questions affecting the world of publicity should find a basic place in an Irish journalistic course.

A forceful, a sympathetic pen can do much to bridge the barrier of misunderstanding between nations, and in the long run relieve suffering humanity of much of its burden.

Literary Map of Ireland

We have an archaeological map of Ireland showing our ancient crosses, cromlechs, castles and abbeys; we have maps illustrating the natural features of the country; maps that show our mineral resources. I remember once seeing in Dublin a library map of Ireland. But nobody has taught of a literary map.

It is true that we have no series of romances in the Scott tradition with a Wicklow mountain setting, but looking at the map of Tipperary, I think we could broadly fix a boundary to the Charles Kickham countryside - the territory and people that have inspired Knocknagow and Sally Cavanagh; the lyric roadside too of his peasant girl "who walked beside the Anner at the foot of Slievenamon."

Going further south to Co. Cork, and with Mallow and Doneraile as landmarks in the priest-novelist's life, we could identify much of the Cannon Sheehan region and trace the wild glens, hills and villages that served as a background to his writing.

In South Tipperary and in Waterford we could transfer to our map the mountain scenery of one of our greatest Gaelic poets, Donnchadh Rua MacConmara. In distant exile he sang of the Comeraghs and Knockmealdowns. It was the noble Comeragh peaks that probably inspired "The Fair Hills of Eire, O!" that has found many translators including Mangan. It is meet, indeed that near their foothills, MacConmara has found a grave.

In Kerry and Limerick it ought to be possible to trace much of the scene of Gerald Griffin's inspiration; while the same writers long verse narrative, "Matt Hyland", would take us back again to Laragh and Glendalough and Luggala.

On our map we could devote "lone Gougane Barra" to the memory of Callanan; we could share the Bog of Allen with Seamus O'Kelly and William Byrne. The Inny River flashes like a thread of silver in Leo Casey's best lyrics; the Erne would go to William

Allingham, while the kingly Shannon enshrines the memory of many of our poets.

It should be easy to trace a boundary around the roads and fields and villages of Goldsmith - Sweet Auburn, the Three Jolly Pigeons, and the world of Dr. Primrose. What of Tom Moore - since all Ireland must be regarded as his territory?

We would have to represent him with special coloured asterisks wherever a place name has given a title to his song. Thus we could identify him with Avoca and Innisfallen and Tara and many other places where beauty, history and legend meet and mingle forever.

Nor would it be difficult to follow Patrick's Pearse's footsteps to Connemara and wander amongst "the little towns of Connacht" to find for our literary map the country of his plays and poems. While I would admit the Aran of the "Riders to the Sea", I would have no place for Synge of the "Playboy" since it is brutally extravagant and false in its essentials to the Western picture. The Donegal of Seamus Mac Manus, the Antrim Glens of Moira O'Neill - every mountain, lake, or valley that has linked itself in song or folk-tale with a novelist or poet's name should be indicated on such a map.

Had Francis Ledwidge never mentioned in his poems such little townlands as Crewbawn or Faughan we would still have evidence from his own pen as to the location of the landscapes of his own poetry. From a European battlefield he wrote to Katherine Tynan:

"You are in Meath now, I suppose. If you go to Tara, go to Rath-na-Righ, and look all around you from the hills of Drumconrath in the north to the plains of Enfield in the south, where Allen Bog begins, and remember me to every hill and wood and ruin, for my heart is there. If it is a clear day you will see Slane Hill, blue and distant...."

Thus our geographical guide to Francis Ledwidge.

Unfortunately, some of our cities have found few true mirrors in the literature of so-called realism. And the maker of the literary map of a country should concern himself only with such writing as interpreted its normal mood and way of life.

For Success in Literature - Armchair or Desk not necessary

From a successful dramatist has just come the strange admission
that he can only write when he is feeling out of sorts and not up to
par generally. I should like to communicate his remarks to the
young man in the suburban villa who told me at the beginning of
the winter that he was about to write his first novel. He believed
that a novel - or a piece of writing of any kind - could only be
perfected in an atmosphere of quietude, armchair luxury and
fireside ease. But, primarily, he believed that if one's best is to go
in to the work there must be perfect health and physical fitness.
And added to all this he should have unlimited spare time.

The annals of literature prove him wrong. Just as with the pines of
the far north where the sterner ice-bound winters tend to produce a
more enduring timber, so art, oftener than not, has flourished in
adversity. Masterpieces of the past - and indeed of all time - have
been produced far outside the centre of fireside comfort or even
the amenities of desk or study. Sentries in the night-watchman's
hut; farm labourers sheltering from the rain; captives in debtor's
prisons; felons in convict settlements - such were the men and the
conditions often associated in the past with great writings.

More trying still. Notable books have been written in the trenches;
in the hospital ward at the base or inside the barbed wire
entanglement of the internment camp.

So much for an atmosphere of ease and quiet! More startling is
the answer to the perfect health argument. "The fine minds", a
notable writer shrewdly remarks, "are generally to be found in
bodies that are constantly on the way to the drug store or family
doctor". He adds that there is not a life insurance company in
existence which would have taken a chance on Shakespeare,
Moliere, Mark Twain, Robert Louis Stevenson, Swift, Samuel
Johnson, Keats, Shelley, and our own Oliver Goldsmith. And
these are but a small number of names taken at random from a
formidable list.

To go into the wider field of the arts one could call to mind
Michelangelo, that frail delicate sculptor-artist, "who was born to

51

paint the sky"; Beethoven, who has made music immortal: Mozart, Chopin, Handel.

In spite of ill-health Elizabeth Barrett Browning achieved fame as a poetess; it was a man far from robust - Edgar Allan Poe - who attained the highest pinnacle in American letters and wrought some of the most exquisite images to be found in the whole range of English poetry.

A hundred handicaps, including want and sickness, did not prevent Mangan from pouring the passion of a nation into the stanzas of "Dark Rosaleen". Nor did his miseries cloud his ecstasy when he caught the true spirit of the Gaelic original:

> *"I walked entranced*
> *Through a land of Morn*
> *The sun, with wondrous excess of light*
> *Shone down and glanced*
> *Over seas of corn*
> *And lustrous gardens aleft and right*
> *Even in the clime*
> *Of resplendent Spain*
> *Beams no such sun upon such a land*
> *But it was the time*
> *Twas in the reign*
> *Of Cathal Mor of the Wine-red Hand".*

Thus can genius, out of an environment of sickness and wretchedness sing with a note of opulence, festivity and health, and indeed with words of a transcending magic.

Another Irishman, Richard Dalton Williams: Could he have written so touchingly of the fragile beauty of the Munster girl dying of consumption in a Dublin hospital were he not aware of the same fatal malady already sealing his own doom. Gerard Griffin has told us, too, that all through his writing career his literary triumphs and laurels were snatched from the very fingers of death.

Are they not a lesson in courage and dauntlessness of spirit those pages and pages of romance falling to the floor as Scotts indefatigable pen raced ceaselessly across the paper in one gallant effort to clear off a debt of several thousand pounds - an obligation which fell upon him through the ill-fortunes of his partner. And at length he succeeds. Or take again, John Boyle O'Reilly on the deck of a prison ship on the Indian Ocean, singing his sweetest songs, knowing all the while that the future held only for him penal servitude and Van Dieman's Land.

Yet with such evidence of art and literature thriving in adverse circumstances, the young writer still aspires to join those (and they make a goodly number too) who have grown to be literary giants both physically and intellectually, and who have still produced masterpieces, notwithstanding the presence of armchairs, fountain pens and typewriters.

Irish Harvest Musings

There is an old Ireland passing away - quietly but surely passing. It is the Ireland of the thatched house, the flail and the scythe. An older Ireland still is already gone - the Ireland of the reaping hook. Four men with hooks reaped an acre of corn in a day. That was in the middle of the last century and earlier. What do we know of manual toil since we know nothing of reaping with a hook?

But the scythe is passing too - the scythe which recalls the spacious and promising years which marked the opening of this century. Amid all the fields of memory the harvest field of my boyhood emerges clear with its cheerful toil, its laughter, and its song. I was remembering it when I wrote :

> "The corn ears droop with heavy grain and dew,
>   The reaping will be pleasant here today,
>   Laughter and girls' song the long hours through
>   Ah, I am sad that I must go away!"

The deliberate, measured gesture of the mower as wave by wave of the golden sea of corn went down before him; the busy hands behind him taking out and shaping the sheaves and, lastly, the womenfolk at the binding. How I remember it all. The character of the binder was always expressed in the bound sheaf. The tidy and thorough housewife who believed in whatever is worth doing at all is worth doing well, certainly registered her conviction in the sheaves she bound. You saw it in her deft sure fashioning of the corn belt and in the tidiness of the finished sheaf which she put from her hand. Not a stray ear remained behind her on the fresh stubble.

And you knew the youth or maiden who took the line of least resistance - their character was in their sheaves also. Loose, careless binding - ears trailing the field - inefficiency. How pleasant was the tea hour towards the end of a warm harvest day. We sat about on the sheaves and how delicious the tea tasted in the open air, not to speak of the home-made bread and the fresh yellow butter. No picnic could equal it.

The particular harvest field I remember looked down from a hillside on a wide stretch of fair country. Everywhere we saw the golden fields with their teams of harvesters. Over all was a mellow sunlight, while towers of sunny cloud floated in slow peace on the shores of the great blue.

What thoughts the harvest day brings to all of us. The millions - yea, countless millions of ripening ears whisper in the wind of God's unbounded goodness to His children in exile. Do we not see in it His blessing on the labours of our hands? The harvest-tide too illustrates the lesson of fulfilment. It reminds us of the life that fulfils its morning promise of nobility and greatness. It brings us thoughts of the "ancient of days", those seven years of plenty when Joseph was ruler in Egypt. It lives in immemorial song and romance recalling

> *"the sad heart of Ruth when sick for home*
> *she stood in tears amid the alien corn."*

And the harvest field white and ready for the reaper will ever be a striking symbol for Catholic youth. For were not His words: "The Harvest indeed is great but the labourers are few".

Thus the harvest fields of Ireland tell of His precious harvest fields in distant lands. The overflowing harvest of souls in Africa, in the East, and everywhere on the continents and islands of the remote seas. No doubt Ireland is ever sending forth brave young toilers, but how few they are in comparison with the mighty harvest.

There are two poignant stanzas in a poem by an Irish poet with which we will conclude our Harvest Musings:

> *"And here they rustle in the sun*   *But Harvest Fields of Pagan lands*
> *These countless shining ears*   *So well the morn may weep*
> *The golden corn-field on which*   *How many priceless ears are there*
> *The morn has shed her tears.*   *That none may ever reap?"*

Fathers of Modern Irish Agriculture - Cistercian Pioneers

Trowel and hammer and the implements of the field will be taken up as if they had been only laid aside yesterday. And yet it is 400 years since a Cistercian monk last worked upon the lands of Mellifont.

With the zeal and enthusiasm of Crusaders they will battle with the soil, drain and fence, crop and till and revolutionise the entire earth of their new dominion.

When the story of the Irish ploughed field and of scientific and systematic tillage comes to be written, it will be found that the pioneering agriculturists were the Cistercian monks of six centuries ago. In a scholarly study of the old Cistercian Abbeys of Ireland of which Mellifont was the earliest, Rev. Professor Power tells us that the monks of these monasteries introduced, amongst other things a new system of agriculture.

"It is to the Cistercian influence", he writes "that we are indebted for first reclamation of fen and woodland; it may indeed be claimed for the white monks that they are the fathers of modern Irish agriculture". And he adds: "How much arterial drainage and road-making we owe to the Cistercians it is now impossible to calculate. Of the thirty-six or so abbeys which the Cistercians founded in Ireland in the twelfth and thirteenth centuries, more than twelve still stand as imposing monuments to their memory. Those commanding ruins - churches, towers and cloisters - incidentally form part of our national and scenic inheritance. One does not find the grace and poetry of Chartres Cathedral, for early Cistercian art had a certain severity as if in keeping with the austere life of the monks. Yet as their buildings developed through later centuries a good deal of ornament was introduced.

One is reminded, if remotely, of the gargoyles and quaint facial expressions of old French architecture in studying these symbolic stone faces that adorn the outer wall of Tintern, one of the two Cistercian Abbeys in Co. Wexford. But of what are some of those faces symbols? If one expresses merriment, another repose, a third is sphinx-like, inscrutable.

If the Franciscans introduced the belfry into church architecture, the Cistercians were the Irish pioneers of stained glass. Whether they had the secret of the wonderful blue and rose windows of Chartres and other mediaeval cathedrals those ruined abbeys and churches cannot now tell. The despoilers of the 16th century had no thought for such things. Recent excavation, however, in some of our Irish Cistercian abbeys has revealed beautiful tiled flooring that had been hidden under the grass and debris of 300 years.

Two of our Cistercian ruins are in the Six Counties, Iniscourcey and Grey Abbey, both in Co. Down. Indeed, most of those ancient monasteries have an historical importance. Rev. Professor Power writes: "No fewer than twelve out of our total thirty six or thirty-seven Cistercian abbeys pre-date the English invasion and an additional twelve are of purely native foundation." Boyle Abbey, he reminds us, contains almost as much native Romanesque as all the other churches of Connacht put together.

The foundation of the Cistercian Abbey of Baltinglass is attributed to Dermot McMurrough, but the patrons of the greater number of those monasteries were Irish chieftains.

The last of those great monasteries to be affected by the Dissolution Decree was Holy Cross in Tipperary. Yet wherever one of those magnificent piles may be seen today, one may trace in the landscape around them the remnants of a well-planned industrial and agricultural activity - mill-ponds and bridges and fish-streams; great gardens where fruit and honey must have been cultivated on a large scale; hill-slopes of forestry and far-extending acres that must at one time have been a golden ocean of corn. The poor and the needy, the pilgrim and the guest found alms or a hospitable table.

But it always must be remembered that in judging the works of Cistercian hands, whether in architecture or in the fields, we see but the externals. The essential Cistercian life has no concern with the things that are Caesar's - lifelong contemplation and prayer and midnight vigil is ever directed ad majorem Dei gloriam.

Mount Melleray, now little more than a century old, marked the beginning of Cistercian Renaissance in Ireland. In 1879 an abbey of the Order was founded at Roscrea. Thus, we have one in Munster, one in Leinster; the New Mellifont in the old province of Ulster will be a third, and it is already rumoured that in time the Order will be extended to Connacht, probably indeed to the vicinity of the great Abbey of Boyle.

If the Cistercian or Trappist methods in the scientific treatment of land, as illustrated on the mountain farm of Melleray, were pursued generally by our people there is many a barren wilderness throughout Ireland that could be a scene of fruitful plenty.

The sweetest sound of the Irish countryside - When the Angelus Bell is ringing

The feast of the Visitation of Our Lady (2nd July) calls up those words so familiar to every Irish heart:

"Behold, the handmaid of the Lord".

An Irish poet whose heart was one with the Irish countryside and who, strangely enough, died in the month of July, fits this line beautifully into a stanza expressive of the atmosphere of an Irish summer evening.

But then, is not the Angelus Bell and the Irish countryside inseparable in any picture, whether the painter be an Irish Millet or an Irish Turner?

Indeed I always associate the opening of that fine poem "The Plougher" by Padraic Colum with the painting by Millet:

"O man standing lone and bowed earthward,
Thy day is a task near its close - give thanks
to the night-giving God."

Here truly we can see the tired worker with bowed head standing above the ploughed earth in the silence and the sunset. Ledwidge, like Colum, has given us perfect glimpses of this aspect of the Irish evening. For besides its great spiritual message, there is poetry and music and rest in the deep tones of the Angelus Bell as they flow in waves of sound over the great silences of the hill, the wood, the bog. They break the stillness of the dewy morning; they divide the noon, and over the stretches of the bog the turfcutters stand in prayer; the mower makes the Sign of the Cross, his hand raised to his perspiring forehead; the soft responses come from the maiden standing above the binding of the sheaf - and so the sweetness, the music, the consolation of the Angelus. It is in verses like Kickham's "Irish Peasant Girl" that the exile will remember with a pang the ringing of the village bell,

59

but perhaps most of all in that lovely little picture-poem "The Harbour". I quote the first and last stanza:

" I think if I lay dying in some land
Where Ireland is no more than just a name,
My soul would travel back to find that strand
From whence it came."

" And then the Angelus - I'd surely see
The swaying bell against a golden sky,
So God Who kept the love of home in me
Would let me die".

What memories are in those lines for the exile far away - aye, maybe far away where the paths of men are Godless and there is no Angelus Bell. Memories....Does he not see again rising clear above the hazes of youth the spire in the trees, its cross against the sky; the pleasant meadows under the low western sun; the little white roads of dusk winding through the hedges of scented hawthorn. The bell rings. It is answered by another bell somewhere amid the hills - and yet by a third - the far, faint, bell of a dreaming town. Or perhaps he hears the bell as I have heard it, its deep wave of sound coming to me over the waters of an Irish lake and up the sunlit evening hillside where I sought the cows at milking time. Hallowed sounds of the Irish countryside, how you follow us over the world! Truly has the poet written of "Mary and Ireland".

"Sweet is thy name, O Mother,
When the Angelus Bell rings clear
In the morning light, in the noontide,
In the evenings of all the year."

The sound the mower makes as he sharpens his scythe is sweet; wild and magical is the voice of nature herself whether her voice is heard in the singing bird or in the running stream; but the Angelus Bell bearing its message over hillside and boreen has the dearest sound of all. Surely, as the spire or the belfry tower point heavenwards those gladdening and hallowed sounds bear our thoughts upwards too, beyond earth and time. They fill the valleys with soothing melody, and they seem to fill the soul too with a great peace.

60

The Hills of '98 (In Co. Wexford)

Nearly all the hills of Co. Wexford figure in the story of 1798, and next month, bonfires will blaze along their crests and the nights will be filled with music. More famous than all the others, two hills stand in the limelight of history. They are Oulart and Vinegar Hill.

It was on Whit Sunday, 1798, that Father John Murphy and his men took up their position on Oulart Hill. He was attacked by the North Cork Militia but his rebel pike men rallied around him to a man and he won the day.

From Oulart Hill one may obtain a fine view of North Co. Wexford, The Blackstairs - Mount Leinster and the distant Wicklow peaks cast their spell upon the landscape as only the mountains of Eire can - ringing the view around with enchantment.

Vinegar Hill, what school child has not heard the name! Less than forty minutes ago I have been on its summit. Beneath it is Enniscorthy and the Slaney and when summer visits our land the fifteen mile river valley from Enniscorthy to Wexford presents us with a picture of romantic loveliness. Enniscorthy, was the next milestone on Father Murphy's roadway of victory and Vinegar Hill marked the last desperate stand of the Wexford men. From its summit one can see clearly all those other hills of '98 - Three Rock over Wexford town; Carrigbyrne westward; and the high country that looks down on New Ross. The journey by rail or river from Enniscorthy to Wexford will unfold for you entrancing vistas of wood and water and castled steep. But a word about Enniscorthy itself which lies in the very shadow of Vinegar Hill. You must not miss visiting its beautiful Cathedral of St. Aidan, the patron of Ferns. There is a fine statue of Father Murphy in the Market Place of the town, overlooking one of its hilly streets, also is a Norman Castle originally built by Raymond le Gros in the thirteenth century. In a subsequent age it was the home of the poet Spencer and later still during the Rising of '98 the Wexford men used it as a prison.

A pleasant little town Enniscorthy with its terraced slopes and climbing streets, and the broad Slaney a-sparkle on its shining sands.

The Mountain of Forth (or the Three Rocks) is yet another of the hills of '98 which will send up its midnight bonfires. This heath clad, rocky highland rises a little to the west of Wexford town and overlooks the barony of the same name - Forth. It also commands a distant view of the Irish Sea, St. George's Channel and the Atlantic.

The Barony of Forth runs towards the extreme south-east corner of Ireland. Some of Eire's first invaders probably settled in its territory, for French, Danish, and Norman names are still plentiful amongst the inhabitants. In some parts of the Barony too, quaint custom and dialect still survive. Up to a generation ago the English of Chaucer was spoken in parts of this district. Withal, names that are Irish of the Irish, - the O'Byrnes, the O'Connors and the Doyles - hold their own in the land of Forth.

One of the most decisive of the battles of '98 was fought on the Three Rocks. A detachment from Father Murphy's encampment on Vinegar Hill had marched on Wexford and took up their position on the Three Rocks just outside the town. A short and sharp engagement with an advance regiment of English troops which had been sent forward from Duncannon, and victory was with the Wexford men who captured all the enemy guns.

And about ten miles westward still and almost midway between New Ross and Wexford is Carrigbyrne. It commands an enchanting view. All the other hills of '98 are visible from its summit. So to are the spires of three of Co. Wexford's principal towns - Wexford itself, Enniscorthy and Ross. And some twelve miles southward is the bright shimmering ocean. Bannow, Baginbun where Strongbow landed, the Hook Peninsula, the Saltee Islands - all come into the historic picture as seen from Carrigbyrne Hill. It was here the men of Wexford mustered under Bagnal Harvey before the battle of Ross - fateful Ross, with its victory piled upon victory and then ruin and defeat! Carrigbyrne, for all its romantic dressings of pine and heather and emerald fern has its thrilling memories dimmed a little with shadow.

There are other Co. Wexford hills of '98, less famous perhaps, but on these also beacons will burn - Kilthomas, Corrigrua, Ferrycarrig, Corbet Hill. And who knows but the pyramid of Mount Leinster will send up its sword of flame if only in memory of a hero whose grave lies at its base - the hero of a song that has gone around the world - "Kelly the Boy from Killann".

The "Bright May Meadows of Shelmalier"

In connection with the '98 celebrations in Co. Wexford during the coming weeks, old songs will be re-sung and perhaps heard again and again in concert and broadcast. Though "Kelly, the Boy from Killann" is known far and wide it contains lines and phrases that have a purely local application and that require a brief word of explanation for the rest of the world. It is the same with some of the other old '98 songs. Not, by the way, that "Kelly of Killann" is an old song by any means. It cannot be more than twenty-five or thirty years old. It is the work of the late P. J. MacCall, who, though a Dublin man, I think, used to spend long vacations in Co. Wexford. In a number of songs - all marked by a certain literary quality and finish - he enshrined the spirit of historic Wexford and the spirit of its countryside.

To commence with, it is not generally known that there is a handsome monument to the memory of Kelly at his native village of Killann, some nine miles north-west of Enniscorthy. In boldly chiselled lettering the memorial tells his epic story.

Now, in the opening stanza of the song we have the phrases "my bold Shelmalier" and "long barrelled gun of the sea".

Shelmalier is a Co. Wexford barony adjoining the Slaney. Analysed and traced to its origin the word means "the sheeling (or home) of the Mylers". Of Norman origin, we find the Myler, or Meyler families thickly scattered throughout Co. Wexford. "Long-barrelled gun of the sea" refers to a special type of fowling piece used in past times by the men of Slaneyside in shooting wild duck along the river and in the reedy marshes near the sea. This long-barrelled duck-gun was used to effect by the "bold Shelmalier" during the '98 Rising.

In the same first stanza of "Kelly of Killann" we have:

> "Goodly news! Goodly news! Do I bring youth of Forth,
> Goodly news shall you hear, Bargy man".

The Barony of Forth runs southward from Wexford town and takes in Carnsore Point, the extreme south-east corner of Ireland. The Barony of Bargy lies immediately west of Forth. The inhabitants of these "English Baronies," as they have been called, are largely descended from the early Welsh and Norman settlers. Old Anglo-Saxon dialect and custom survived here until recent times. Even still one could compile a small dictionary of quaint words and phrases in everyday use in these Baronies. Withal the men of Forth and Bargy, having in patriotism become more Irish than the Irish themselves, fought bravely in the Rising. One of their distinguished leaders was Captain Bagnal Harvey, of Bargy Castle, who was afterwards executed in Wexford. In the same song ("Kelly of Killann") Mount Leinster is mentioned. This is the highest peak of the Blackstairs, which divides Wexford from Carlow. Southward it looks down on Killann.

In another '98 song, "The Croppy Boy" we have the line,

"In Geneva Barracks the young man died".

It is reasonable enough to think of the beautiful city of the League of Nations and of the Swiss lakes, and hard enough to imagine "Geneva" Barracks in Ireland! But, yes, it is in the Co. Waterford and here is how the name originated. Midway between Waterford and the sea, and on the bank of the joint rivers Barrow, Suir and Nore are the ruins of New Geneva. Here, towards the end of the 18th century (in 1785 to be exact) a colony of Genevese settled. Probably on account of their skill in gold and silver craftsmanship the Irish Parliament facilitated them by a grant of £50,000, a generous sum. Yet it seems the colony did not develop, for we read that "after a few years New Geneva dwindled and died". During the memorable year of '98 the English military, converted the remaining walls of this "Swiss settlement into a fortress or barracks. The ruins of Geneva Barracks may be seen to this day".

The Wexford Priests of '98

Pen picture of Father John Murphy and Father Redmond -
Priest who saved Napoleon's life

In an Irish periodical recently a writer referred the statue in Arklow to the famous Father Murphy of '98. Yes, it is to a Father Murphy of '98 - but not the famous Father John Murphy.

It will be of interest just now to give a few particulars about the Wexford priests of '98, as they are to be found in the more detailed records of the period.

So to commence with Father John. In a footnote to Father Kavanagh's "Insurrection of 1798" he is described as of rather small stature, but of uncommon strength and activity; of such a perfect constitution of body, that though he exposed himself to every hardship, he was never known to suffer from the least illness. He excelled in all manly exercises in which he took great delight and was reputed the best ball player in the parish. His mind was like his body, vigorous and powerful - he won the degree of Doctor of Divinity in the famous College of Seville in Spain. The gentleness and amiability of his disposition together with his other excellent qualities of mind and body endeared him exceedingly to his parishioners.

So much for this intimate pen-picture. When a life of this brave priest comes to be written, it will be seen that primarily Father Murphy was a man of peace - counselling his flock against physical force. Indeed, he hoped against hope that in time the policy of the English Government would be tempered with justice and mercy. But instead (to quote from Monsignor D'Alton's History) "Across the mountains from Wicklow, Carlow and Kildare came tales of fearful cruelty, of flogging and torture, and of no quarter been given in battle. It was said that Orangemen declared that they would wade ankle-deep in Papist blood. It was what the people feared, much more than what they saw which made them United Irishmen; they thought it was better to fall fighting than to be massacred".

Thus the storm was only preparing to burst with a more horrifying intensity, the foreign reign of rapine and terror was extending. And in the very act of peace - of voluntarily handing up their arms - the Insurgents were mercilessly set upon by the Orange Yeomen with fatal effect. The homes of Boolavogue were burning, and it was at this stage that Father John Murphy entered the scene. The young men of Co. Wexford rallied around him in their thousands, and his victories at Oulart and Vinegar Hill belong to history. But "a dismal cloud overcast all the hopes of the Insurgents" when their loved leader fell into the enemy's hands and was ignominiously hanged in the streets of Tullow.

Father Michael Murphy (whose memorial is at Arklow) also comes into the story of '98. We first hear of him in the march on Enniscorthy when leading a number of young men from his own parish of Ballycanew, he joined Father John at a place called Balliorrell. Later, at the battle of Arklow, and just as he was leading his troops to victory, he was shot dead. Immediately his followers lost courage and the town remained in English hands.

Another priest of '98 is Father Philip Roche. He was executed in Wexford, whither he went with the hope of coming to terms with the English leader, General Lake. Of him it has been written "Many Protestants owed their life to his intercession", and Father Kavanagh, the '98 historian adds: "The same may be said with perfect truth of all the other priests who took an active part in the Insurrection".

And history tells of the courage and heroism of Father Corrin in the cause of peace and mercy. It was shortly after the capture of Wexford by the rebel forces - but here is how Joyce's History tells of it :-

"While they occupied the town, a fellow named Dixon on the rebel side, the Captain of a small coasting vessel, who had never taken any part in the real fighting - one of those cruel, cowardly natures sure to turn up on such occasions - collected a rabble, not of the townspeople, but of others who were there from the surrounding districts, and plying them with whisky, broke open the "jail" and "in spite of the expostulations of the more respectable leaders, the mob brought a number of the prisoners to the bridge, and after a mock trial began to kill them one by one. A number, variously stated from forty to ninety, had been murdered, and another batch were brought out, when, according to contemporary accounts, a young priest, Father Corrin, returning from some parochial duties, and seeing how things stood, rushed in at the risk of his life and commanded the executioners to their knees. Down they knelt instinctively when in a loud voice he dictated a prayer which they repeated after him - that God might show to them the same mercy that they were about to show to their prisoners; which so awed and terrified them that they immediately stopped the executions.

Forty years afterwards, continues the historian, Captain Kellett, one of the Protestant gentlemen he (Father Corring or Curran) had saved, followed with sorrow and reverence the remains of that good priest to the grave".

Lastly, the story is told of the execution of Father Redmond P.P. of Ferns, whose sole efforts were directed towards the prevention of outrage. It is said that by the order of Hunter Gowan he was hanged on Gorey Hill.

Of special interest is the record which tells us of Father Redmond's student days in France when he saved the life of no less a person than Napoleon. The students were spending the summer vacation in Bas Poicton. Napoleon was staying there at the time and one day he joined them on a shooting expedition. In attempting to jump over a deep brook, he slipped and fell in. The record says "He was almost drowned when Father Redmond presented his fowling-piece to him (having first discharged it), and thus rescued from ignoble death the man who afterwards ruled half the world".

Historic River Slaney - Christian before Patrick

The most historic of Irish rivers will reflect the light and pageant of past events within a few weeks time. For not only does the Slaney flow past some of the chief battlefields of '98, but recent scholarship has shown that it is the most important river in Irish history. It was not by the Boyne or the Shannon, or the Liffey the Milesians first entered Ireland, but by the Slaney. And it was at Inbher Slainghe the Gospel was first preached in Ireland by St. Ibar, prior to the coming of St. Patrick. How often, too, has this river contributed the setting of the subsequent drama of our country in which Dane and Norman played such a fateful part.

Who was Slainghe? King or Warrior, fable or reality? Who knows? The river that has borne his name through the centuries flows out of a land of beauty. Fain would they hold it captive - those blue Wicklow peaks - Lugnaquilla - awe-inspiring and at times darkly mysterious as a Tibetan mountain. The young Slaney sparkles through the Glen of Imaal. Round its very cradle are memories of Red Hugh and Michael Dwyer.

Baltinglass and the hills again and those grey Cistercian walls that Dermot McMurrough built (some of the records suggest that he is buried here). Tullow, the arena in which Father John Murphy fell to the human wolves and now near the Wexford border at Bunclody the Slaney is back again into a land of mountains. True, they stand a little way apart reflecting in their moods and colours, the ever-changing day - and memories of '98 on the battle streets of Bunclody but ending in defeat for the Wexford men.

So the Slaney winds leisurely through the fertile lands, reflecting the furze blossoms and the branching marigold, and at Enniscorthy the memories begin to crowd thick and fast. The separated centuries seem to nod to one another across the river - the distant days of St. Aidan and the subsequent centuries of the conquering hosts, Raymond le Gros and de Prendergast and the castle where the poet Spenser lived - the fortress which was a prison in '98;

while directly above the town is Vinegar Hill's green crest of victory.

Lyric genius alone could pay tribute to the charm of the Slaney Valley in some of its stretches between Enniscorthy and Wexford, as the embowered river unfolds vista after vista. It was Stephen Gwynn, I think, in one of his delightful books about Ireland, who attracted our attention to the unique and colourful bird life amongst the reeds by the Slaney.

Beyond those reeds and trees is the neighbouring castle of Macmine, the birthplace of a Catholic poetess of considerable gifts - Miss Emily Hickey. She was well known in the literary life of London and was founder of the Browning society (and, by the way, like Spenser, Leigh Hunt during his soujourn in Ireland also, lived by the Slaney.)

Standing sentry on either bank and in unbroken salute as the river rushes past, two towers crown the steeps of Ferrycarrig. Furze bloom and ivy climb precipices, and you may be lucky enough to be here at a time when the fishermen busy with their nets, are drawing from the Slaney some of its silver harvest.
Ferrycarrig must certainly have been one of the first castles the Normans built after setting foot on our shores. The winds of time have dealt kindly with it, and our road-builders of today have taken steps to preserve the very rocks on which it stands.

Easily one of the most enchanting views in Ireland is obtainable from a by-road midway between Ferrycarrig and the village of Castlebridge. This would be from the north bank of the river. The Slaney, broadening beneath us under tree and verdure into a great lake, must suggest to the world traveller a Swiss or Italian loveliness. This must have been the very lake - and not Wexford harbour itself - that O'Ceirin, the 10th century poet, had in mind when he wrote "King of loughs is this lough in the south."
And where Inver Slainghe mingles with the waters of the bay stands Loch Garman herself, with her quaint continental streets and her red sandstone spires - a town so old that origins can scarce be traced in the midst of antiquity.

An Irish Island of Our Lady

A woman of the district, middle-aged, darkly attired, has just finished her pilgrimage. Head bowed in prayer she kneels before the statue of Mary - a touching scene in a setting of pastoral sea and sunlight, while over beyond these inland marine waters the widespread stooks of the barley tell of an abundant land.

Now she has arisen reverently, slowly, and is making her way homeward over the soft green carpet of the island... Yes, she realises I am a stranger, and she is all the more anxious to tell me everything. "The last procession was the greatest ever held, a wonderful procession, thanks be to God". This Island of Our Lady is in the extreme south-east corner of Ireland giving its name to the Parish of Lady's Island, Co. Wexford. There are pilgrims who pray at its shrines and take water from its holy wells associating its name with that of Lourdes or Lough Derg.

It can hardly be called an "island". There are tall and imposing statues of Our Lady standing on an altar. If the authenticity of an apparition be ever established, the statue at the seaward end of the peninsula, erected 38 years ago, will probably have a significance as to place and date. In this image Our Lady is represented with gently flowing hair, while in the statue on the landwards side, she is wearing a crown of gold. On the altar beneath her is engraven the lettering "The Queen of the Island". It is here the pilgrim starts in making a "round" of the island, which includes also a visit to the holy well nearby.

This inland peninsula has for centuries been associated with the name of the Blessed Virgin. It has, too, an historic interest. On the island may be seen the ruins of an ancient church; a Norman castle and, strangest of all, portion of a stronghold or abbey which is a leaning tower of Pisa on a small scale. It would seem as if by some violence or eruption this gable or tower had at some time been uprooted from its foundations and pushed over almost to the point at which it should fall, and in this position it has stoutly remained.

A window in this ruin is an object of great interest to visitors. It is in the shape of an inverted cross. An inhabitant told me that according to one respected theory, it symbolised the death of St. Peter who was crucified head downwards. Lady's Island has also pre-Patrician associations in its old cemetery of St. Ibar - a name that takes us back to the very dawn of Irish history. Beauty, too, pays its tribute to this island of peace. A procession of swans - I counted no less than twenty-one - moved with a slow grace along the marine waters. The same virginal brightness of swan and cloud and ocean air is even reflected in these artificial tributes that human hands strive to pay. For the surrounding cottages and homesteads harmonise with all other symbols in snow-white wall and bower of bloom.

Exquisite beauty, too, very appropriately marks the workmanship of the Church of the Assumption, Lady's Island. It is one of the loveliest edifices in the land especially its interior design. Above the main windows and just beneath the ceiling the symbolism in the Litany of the Blessed Virgin is illustrated wonderfully in stained glass. An entire window is devoted to each symbolic salutation. The tall spire of the church fitly dominates the village, the flower-bright walks and the sun-clear island beyond with its several shrines and ruins.

The extreme south-east end of Ireland - where the Irish Sea and the Atlantic meet in the waters of St. George's Channel is less than two miles distant.

Relics of Famous Irishmen - O'Connell, Meagher, Redmond, Pearse

Out of the May landscapes of Kildare I walked into a world of many times and lands. Quaint broad hats that told of scorching suns over the Gulf of Mexico; Flemish illuminated script of the sixteenth century and beauty that mediaeval hands had wrought in alabaster.

Four hundred years ago a vein of this precious mineral was discovered in the South of England and out of it were fashioned artistic religious plaques which were exported to France and Spain. One of these was presented to a Jesuit, Father Betagh, in 1773, and now a rare and valued possession, indeed, it is one of the treasures of the Museum of Clongowes Wood College, Co. Kildare.

But it is not the chief treasure. No. Father Fergal McGrath, S.J., the Rector of Clongowes, who so kindly conducted me through the College Museum, took me first to see a wonderful crosier of the Middle Ages which was dug up in the Bog of Allen! One could devote much space to a description of this valuable exhibit alone, which is a lasting tribute to the craft and workmanship of past centuries. But then there are so many objects of interest - especially of Irish literary and historical interest - attracting our attention on all sides.

What struck me about this museum at Clongowes is its association with the various Irish movements of the last century and a half. It has memories of the United Irishmen - of Hamilton Rowan (who by the way, tradition has it, narrowly escaped capture or death at the hands of the '98 militia in this very college, which was then Castle Brown. Father McGrath showed me what is believed to be the marks of the pellets in an oak door above the entrance hall of the College.)

Dan O'Connell's hat is on exhibition - strangely picturesque to twenty century eyes. (And here again is a fact of great interest. It was in the old chapel at Clongowes, where Mass is still celebrated, that the Liberator was kneeling in prayer when the news was brought to him that the Emancipation Bill had been introduced into the House of Commons.)

The '48 Movement is well represented in a manuscript poem by Thomas Davis - I saw there "The Vow of Tipperary" - letters by Charles Gavan Duffy and his contemporaries, and a unique photograph group which includes Smith O'Brien and Thomas Francis Meagher, together with their signatures. There is also a letter by Charles Lever.

The hat of Terence Bellew MacManus, which hangs beside O'Connell's, takes us to the Fenian Movement of '67, and most interesting of all is that coveted exhibit which represents that eventful week of our own country with its strange mingling of tragedy and triumph. It is the hat which Padraic Pearse wore on the morning of his execution.

Here is its story. It was picked up by a member of the firing party who gave it to the housekeeper at Kilmainham. She handed it to a policeman who was on duty at Kingsbridge Station; he gave it to Mr. Floyd, now Traffic Manager of the Great Southern Railways, and Mr. Floyd presented it to the Museum of Clongowes Wood College.

We have abundant samples too of Pearse's handwriting in the examination papers which he himself set at Clongowes.

An old playbill of the College dated 1874 announces "Hamlet" with John Redmond in the title role.

So much for a few of the outstanding items of Irish interest. There is a rare volume - a devotional work which belonged to the Old Pretender - and how this book came into the museum after passing through many hands makes a romantic story in itself. A unique treasure is a copy of the New Testament used by St. Ignatius of Loyola, founder of the Jesuit Order, and there is also a Chalice veil used by St. Francis Borgia, third General of the Society of Jesus.

Memories of saints and kings, poets and warriors, statesmen and writers are everywhere recalled. But then has not Clongowes itself the same memories throughout its halls and playgrounds? What makers of Irish history studied here during the past century or more. Their photographs line its galleries - illustrious names that have been a glory to Church and State. But is not the building in which I found this wonderful museum set in a landscape of history with its memories of Queen Maeve and Conal Cearnach and that green grave at Bodenstown.

Wanted - A Catholic Poetry Renaissance

It has long been the hope of the present writer to see a great Renaissance in Catholic poetry, in Ireland, in England, in America, and throughout the world. While the present century was still young, Francis Thompson's tremendous poem "The Hound of Heaven" caused the intellectual world to close the page upon Swinburne and the other Victorians, and so experience the full thrill of a great Catholic poet.

Mr. Robert Lynd endorses an old conviction of mine when he writes: "In my opinion, a religious background, either expressed or implied, will always be necessary to the production of great literature. Everywhere the imaginative man, confronted with the mystery of life and death, is forced to adopt a religious attitude to life - the attitude of awe before the eternal mysteries. Without it there can be neither the greatest poetry nor the greatest prose. Great poetry will cease to be written when poets will cease to be men for whom the invisible world exists."

Now when I speak of a Catholic Poetry Renaissance I do not necessarily imply devotional verse only. I include the nature poems of Francis Ledwidge and the love poems of Alice Meynell. I lay special stress on those poems by Catholic poets that would have the widest intellectual appeal in non-Catholic circles - poetry that would have the same influence on the sceptic as Newman's prose had on Hardy and Gosse. For, when all is told, it is the Catholic poet, whether he is singing of the meadows, or the skies, of love or memory, of childhood or death, who can soar into the loftiest realms of beauty - because beauty to him holds always the promise of still greater beauty to come.

What I have said somewhere before does not lose in repetition. If there is not a sempiternal hope in one's heart there is nothing. He who holds that oblivion follows life - or even he who is without that certainty which Faith brings - has nothing to inspire him to high endeavour. Even in his temporary world, the stars that sang together on the morning of creation, the illimitable wastes of ocean, and the pines voicing the saga of the centuries, cannot produce in his soul "the great thrill" which is germane to all immortal writing.

For those things, according to his pagan belief, must be less transient than human life, the ultimate end of which is dust!

If a Renaissance cannot come yet in the output of good Catholic poetry, we can at least make known much that has already been written and that at present exists only for the few. That precisely is what the London Catholic Poetry Society is doing. It is by poetry recitals that we can best reveal the beautiful soul of Alice Meynell, one of the world's immortal women. Her "San Lorenzo's Mother", that won the admiration of such critics as Ruskin, and her "Shepherdess", the beloved of anthologists, are amongst the lovely things that we want to make known.

There are many other poets of modern times through whom our Catholic culture has expressed itself in song. One has only to glance at the names associated with the Society I have mentioned - Alfred Noyes, G.K. Chesterton, Katherine Tynan, Sheila Kay-Smith, Padraic Colum and numerous others.

How few are acquainted with Dowson's "Nuns of Perpetual Adoration" -

"And it is one with them when evening falls
And one with them the cold return of day."

In the pages of Francis Ledwidge we find:

"Night tells her Rosary of Stars."

And again:

"When I am on the wide seas for other lands,
Won't you remember me with folded hands,
And keep me happy in your pious prayer."

This is the remembrance that a great poet asks of his love; for the spiritual world is ever near.

In Chesterton's "House of Christmas", Bethlehem and what it means is revealed to the world in quite a startling way. In that strong robust Chestertonian strain, yet delicate at times with the pensiveness that almost brings a tear we are given:

> *"To an open house in the evening*
> *Home shall men come*
> *To the place where God was homeless*
> *And all men are at home."*

There come to us out of the past the voices of Lionel Johnson and Coventry Patmore and poor Joyce Kilmer:

> *"Dead in his youthful prime*
> *Never to laugh nor love again,*
> *Nor taste the summertime."*

In modern years one notices the big daily newspapers welcoming oftentimes a spiritual note in verse. This is indicative of much. Our uneasy world is realising more than ever that Wall Street does not hold everything we desire.

In the "New York Times", that great organ of hustling America, I read recently a tender little poem entitled "The Postulant". It has such stanzas as:

> *"There is no proof I've walked the world around,*
> *I have roused no love that has not reached its end,*
> *I have built no house on any solid ground,*
> *I have made no solemn vow to any friend.*
>
> *Give me the mourning garments, cut my hair,*
> *God of my dreamy youth, I have heard Thy call,*
> *Lean to me once again, though I bring no prayer,*
> *My silence and my tears will tell Thee all."*

This is just to illustrate the tendency to which I refer.

A Catholic Poetry Renaissance can have its beginnings in what is already written. Let us search and sift and exhibit our jewels. In one line of magic, the poet may uncurtain unimagined worlds showing the doubting wayfarer where he may find at last the "land of Heart's Desire."

It was in the song that the Israelites voiced their sorrow by the willows of Babylon; it was in song that the victory of nations was proclaimed; and it is in song that we can best hint of that "Light Invisible" towards which the Church bids us turn our eyes.

Search for a Lost Treasure of Ancient Ireland

The sun never sets on the far-flung activities of our race, and at the moment, while political and economic questions near home claim our attention, a search of Irish cultural importance is being made on the other side of the world.

An Irish priest is endeavouring to trace in Australia the lost book of Clonenagh.

Our Irish illuminated MSS have had strange adventures; the Book of Armagh, down the long centuries of its existence, passed through many hands before finding its way into Trinity College. After the Danish wars the world famous Book of Kells was found hidden in a bog with its gold bindings much damaged; and strangest of all, the manuscript of Lindisfarne, now in the British Museum, was once recovered from the bottom of the Irish Sea.

Of the vicissitudes of the book of Clonenagh, we know little, but if it comes to light it may revive an interest in that hallowed countryside by the Slieve Bloom Mountains whence it takes its name. It was at Clonenagh, some four miles south-west of Portlaoighise, we had one of the great schools of early Christian Ireland. Clonenagh, or Cluain Eidnech means the "Ivy Meadow" - a name suggested by the trailing ivy in those dense forests of ancient days.

St. Fintan, the founder of Clonenagh, was of the race of Conn of the Hundred Battles, and therefore, distantly related to Columcille, who was his contemporary. It was on the eastward slope of Slieve Bloom that he intended to found his school, but, directed by Providence, he chose the oak-girdled glade of Clonenagh, a little way from the mountains base.

One of his illustrious pupils was Comgall of Bangor, who was afterwards to found a famous school on the shore of Belfast Lough - an academy that more than any other in our land was destined to influence profoundly the entire future of European culture. For it will be recalled that one of the scholars of Bangor was

Columbanus, a name of continental magnitude, with special importance for the French and Italian peoples.

To return to the lost "Book of Clonenagh", will it throw further light on the personality of Aengus - justly termed the Ceile De, or "Servant of God"?   As long as the morning sun lights Slieve Bloom and the eastward levels of Laoighis his name will be remembered in the sacred poetry of the Gael.   Born in this countryside about the middle of the eighth century, his scholarship and educational attainments stand as a lasting tribute to his Alma Mater - the School of Clonenagh.   Even though his reputation for learning spread through the whole land of Eire, Aengus chose the way of the hermit with its attendant hardships and austerities. Yielding, however, to the counsel of Maelruain, the Abbot of Tallaght Monastery, near Dublin, Aengus decided to utilise his intellectual gifts and devote his scholarship to the glory of God and the honour of Ireland.   It was in co-operation with Maelruain that he compiled the famous "Martyrology of Tallaght" - a catalogue in prose of the Irish Saints.   The oldest copy of this MS is embodied in the Book of Leinster.

It is recorded that it was as the result of a vision by the old Church of Coolbangher, near Portarlington, where he saw a host of angels around a newly made grave, that Aengus the Culdee wrote his Feilire.   He learned from the local priest that a soldier who had just died would be buried in this grave.   Aengus, who alone had seen the vision asked if the man's life had been marked by any outstanding virtues or graces, and the priest said it was his daily habit to invoke the intercession of all the saints whom he could call to mind.

In a poetic diction, not unworthy of the later Francis of Assisi, Aengus the Culdee enshrined the memory of all the saints of the Church and this Feilire, or Festology of Aengus is regarded as the most valuable of the Irish ecclesiastical writings that have come down to us from those distant times.

His work not only merited the approval of the royal bard of Ireland, but won his unstinted praises.

Many other literary works, too, are attributed to Aengus and there is evidence in the ancient writings of his deep love for the pleasant country-side of his childhood and for the "cold, pure Nore" where, on the first stages of its journey, it sets forth from the shadow of Slieve Bloom. According to the "Leabhar Breac" his grave is at Clonenagh, his beloved Cluain Eidnech of the many crosses. A complete copy of his "Martyrology of Tallaght", more exhaustive that that in the "Book of Leinster" is the property of the Belgian Government. It is preserved in the Burgundian Library at Brussels, and is the work of Brother Michael O'Clery, one of the Four Masters. And now the "Book of the Ivy Meadow", with which the name of St. Aengus is at least remotely associated, is believed to be somewhere in distant Australia. How far-scattered are Ireland's MSS and treasures of the past.

How do you reply to a tourist ?

Everybody in Ireland should be a tourist's guide. Not officially or commercially, but out of enthusiasm and love for that regional Irish earth that is one's native land.

How often does the foreign tourist slow down his car to ask a passer-by, or perhaps a road-mender, or a farmer in the fields, for brief information about that old tower, or ruin on the neighbouring hillside? And how often is he told that it is just Ballymurphy Castle, or the reply may be: "Oh, that old tower - that old tower in Kellaghan's field - I never heard it called anything, sir, only Kellaghan's tower".

And that is all there is to tell about the last fragment of a Norman keep, even though the county historian may have devoted a lengthy chapter to its story. Thus, the tourist goes his way ignorant of the Kings and Crusaders, the colour and glamour associated with that grey ruin, because his informant has not familiarised himself with the story. Never even heard of it !

Or that great Abbey seen from the carriage window. The visitor is impressed by its imposing magnificence. He is told that it is Dunbrody Abbey. And here its story ends. How few can add, off-hand, that it is the Abbey of St. Paul, that it is standing there almost since the Norman Invasion and that its original Charter is in the Bodleian Library, Oxford. Everybody in South Wexford should be able to tell the tourist that this Abbey ruin of Dunbrody is considered the finest, not only in the county, but in all Ireland; just as the Meathian should be in a position to state at once that the Yellow Steeple, Trim, is Ireland's tallest remnant of Norman masonry.

A little more than the bare name of a cairn, a cromlech, or a rath would make all the difference to the enquiring holidaymaker. A little-known lake may be enchanting, but that enchantment will be deepened if the traveller, who comes upon it unaware, can learn casually from the passer-by that its origin is associated with a beautiful legend. And if you know the legend, do not be long-winded in the telling, or you will only succeed in boring your listener.

An answer to a question - if you know the answer - costs nothing.   And there is no reason why everybody who can read and write should not steep himself in authentic local history.   It will be an act of patriotism if you are able to reveal a new fact of glory on any object that attracts the visitor's eye, and on which he may have already some general guide book enlightenment.

Often too the tourist listens with a less prejudiced mind to the fresh, spontaneous reply of the local resident.   He is tired of the monotonous intoning of many of the guides and vergers that have shown him over the cathedrals and tombs of foreign cities, of the chain of glaring and gross inaccuracies that is sometimes retailed to him through ignorance of religious ritual.

Try as far as possible to have your information correct;   the county libraries all stock the standard works on their respective regions.   And let brevity and courtesy mark any help that you can give the tourist.   We are all sharers of a common national heritage - a cultural inheritance that rivals that of Greece and Rome.   But the stones of antiquity lie dead until those who love them are able to give to them a living voice.

I have been singularly fortunate in meeting people in various parts of Ireland who knew their regional story and who could speak enlighteningly and intelligently on every landmark in their surroundings.   There was the Wexford man who pointed out to me with a disarming dogmatism the exact cove where Strongbow landed;   the Clare boatman who, in a stanza of folk song, called up the glowing story of his territory;   the man in the Midland meadow who talked with a real enthusiasm of his native village and not merely of its antiquities, but of its scholars, its poets and its literary men.   He could even quote appreciatively from their more ambitious writings.

Against this there is the story of the old man in Co. Waterford who did not give much help, though he unintentionally entertained and

amused his visitor.   The tourist stopped to ask abut Lismore, the
famous city of St. Carthage.

"Aye, Lismore was a great place for saints and scholars", said the
old man, "and at that time it was all wan long street;   the saints
lived on wan side of the street and the scholars on the other."

In St. Brigid's country
The Round tower of Kildare - A Symbol

If you mention the Liffey, the average person who knows Dublin will at once think of the river that flows past the quays, O'Connell Bridge, the Customs House, never of the other Liffey that winds serenely through deep grassy meadows, and under broad woodland bridges. Indeed the Liffey where it flows through Kildare might well bear the joint names of St. Patrick and St. Brigid. Their missionary paths meet and part and interlace here. Their personalities have left on the plain of Magh Life an influence that is holy, vital and everlasting. But who was Life, whose half-legendary memory lives in the river's wave? Was she after all but a princess of fable?

There have been many moons and many winters since first I tramped that pleasant country that lies on either side of Liffey's banks over which the long blue line of the Wicklow Mountains keeps distant guard. The footsteps of our National Apostle have been traced along the entire riverside in cross and ruin and holy well. While essentially this is Brigid's country - the land of her beloved oak tree, the Curragh over which she drove in her chariot, the meadows in which she tended her flocks.

When I re-visited Kildare town recently I tried to reconstruct the long vanished picture of St. Brigid's city. The Round Tower - the tallest in Ireland - dominates the village and the surrounding plain. And yet may not this inspiring monument date from Brigid's very day. After consulting the various authorities on our round towers, I find Wakeman giving his unqualified support to Dr. Petrie in his conclusions. Here they are:

1. That the towers are of Christian and ecclesiastical origin and were erected at various periods between the fifth and thirteenth centuries.

2. That they were designed to answer, at least, a two-fold use, namely to serve as belfries, and as keeps or places of strength, in which the sacred utensils, books, relics and other valuables,

were deposited and into which the ecclesiastics to whom they belonged could retire for security in case of sudden attack.

3. That they were probably also used, when occasion required, as beacons and watch towers.

To return to No. 1. "of Christian and ecclesiastical origin and erected at various periods between the fifth and thirteenth centuries". If it does not actually date from Brigid's time, the tower must surely have been built in the hey-day of the great school which she founded. So even if the oak tree has long since fallen with age, and the sacred fire has been put out by the reformers, this tower still stands mightily in the midst of our concrete and tarmac age. It stands as a symbol of the solidity of things done at Kildare.

Lingering beside that age-grey column fortress-like in its strength, one thinks back across the gulf of centuries to Brigid. Regarding her from a human standpoint, or as a historical personage, she emerges as one of the greatest women of all history - "the woman with the Papal mind"; Brigid who was the same fibre as Teresa of Avila and Catherine of Sienna; Brigid the organiser, the counsellor, the adviser - and, above all, the worker. With this tower as a symbol of strength and dignity and perfection we can readily let our imagination reconstruct around it the vanished city of prayer and action. We see St. Conleth, the craftsman in metal, with students flocking around him from far and near. Book rests, bells, illuminated manuscripts - the busy fingers of the artists and artificers were at work in the great school of Kildare. Weaving and embroidery, penmanship, music and poetry, and last but not least agricultural and pastoral activities. And it is here again that St. Brigid, in the gentler role of shepherdess, comes vividly to life. For as Miss Alice Curtayne writes "Everyone knows that she is supremely the saint of agricultural life. Even when she was the Mother Abbess of all the nuns of Ireland, she seems to have gone on milking cows, making butter, cheese and home-brewed ale until the end. She is, therefore, different from all possible modern counterparts in that she fostered with equal intensity, learning, culture and pastoral pursuits."

Sculpture; ornamental architecture; we have only to turn and examine the tower, the artistry of its doorway, the mouldings, to realise another branch of the work that has been done at ancient Kildare. Even in the days of Cambrensis, Brigidine legends hung about this tower. And as we leave the village of Kildare and travel northwards through the Curragh and the plain of Magh Life we look around us at the never-changing face of Brigid's countryside. There is royal Allen, black against the last light of evening; the Wicklow range soon to disappear in the deepening dusk. As a biographer reminds us, Brigid's memory is associated with all these dewy spaces around us. As the writer says "Even the bleating of a sheep in the dusk instantly evokes the rumble of her chariot wheels, and the sense of her benediction descending on the land."

A beautiful thought. And at Newbridge the plain of Magh Life takes us once more to the river itself - a river that more than any other in our land should be named after the Patron and Patroness of the Gael.

Past Glories of Beautiful Adare

Somewhere back amongst the crowding years lies that sky-clear morning when I walked southwards from Mungret College and Patrick's Well and over the Maigue into Adare. Though I have seen many another Irish village like Newtownbarry and Blessington and Clonmellon with their tree-green streets of quiet beauty, I always felt that Adare was the most beautiful village in Ireland, though I share the opinion of Mr. Dermod O'Brien, R.H.A., that the place has an English aspect, due I think to its reflecting the orderliness and decorum of the neighbouring Dunraven demesne.

Had William Wordsworth entered Adare he would certainly retrace his steps a little to where a bridge crosses the silver river. For here by the water, amid trees and pastoral antiquities, is the immemorial Adare - the vale that may indeed have influenced the contemplative verse of Gerald Griffin and Aubrey de Vere.

In this monastic meadow lies the dust of bishops and princes. Here too is the tomb of Thomas, Earl of Kildare, and of his wife, a daughter of the Earl of Desmond who died on the feast of St. Anthony, 1486. Early in that century they had built for the Franciscans the monastery of Adare. Raymond de Burgh, the last Bishop of Emly - before the See was united to Cashel - is also buried here.

The grass has long since grown over the footprints of Franciscan feet, and the great deeds and sacrifices that inspired the "Book of Adare" seem to belong more to legend than to history; yet legend they are not, for the name of this monastic centre was once known across Europe, south to the Mediterranean and beyond the borders of Asia.

For early in the 13th century, and two hundred years before the sons of St. Francis came to Adare, an Abbey was founded here which of its kind was unique in Ireland. Its community was a branch of the Trinitarian Order, which devoted its activities to the ransoming of Christian captives from the Saracens. Indeed, this noble aim seemed largely to have been its raison d'etre.

"In the year 1230", writes Father Bonaventure Baron, the distinguished Franciscan scholar "during the pontificate of Gregory IX, the Order of Trinitarians was introduced to Ireland. The splendid monastery of Adare was erected by the Earls of Kildare who endowed it with ample revenues.

"The Fathers of that House devoted themselves to the object of their institute - the redemption of captives - so earnestly, that some were found who not only sold their lands but their silver plate - nay and their chalices - to supply the necessary funds.

"The nobles of the country, and the people, gave the Trinitarians considerable sums of money. At the time of the first redemption, for which six of the principal magnates of Ireland made large advances, the Earl of Desmond contributed the entire of his table service, great part of which was solid gold and the remainder silver gilt. The Countess gave her rich gold bracelets and her ear rings set with stones of priceless value, nay, all her ornaments, for the same pious purpose.

At that time the Saracens were making frequent descents upon the shores of the Mediterranean and carrying off hosts of Christian prisoners to Tunis and Algiers. It is recorded that the Trinitarians of Adare ransomed no less than 6,300 captives. Further, many of the Irish priests of Adare, in pursuit of this same high purpose, shed their martyr blood on the sands of Egypt and Palestine. In this role of glory we find the names of Father Arthur O'Neill, Provincial of the Trinitarians in Ireland, and Father Thaddeus O'Higgins..

"Of all our Munster monasteries there was none more beautiful than that of Adare", wrote a Franciscan chronicler of the 16th century. Its setting must certainly have contributed much to its beauty as it did to the Trinitarian foundation of centuries earlier."

Writing too, of this rich countryside of the Geraldines, Thomas Davis reminds us:

> *"What gorgeous shrines, what Brehon lore, what minstrel feasts were there*
> *In and around Maynooth's grey keep and palace-filled Adare"*

Flowing Shannon-wards under summer trees the Maigue still echoes the minstrel's music and the poet's song.

Seaside Shrines of the Decies

Just a name on the map to most readers. Ardmore, a seaside village on the extreme south-west coast of Co. Waterford has again been chosen by Muintir na Tire for its congress, which this time is of an international character.

One of these days this watering place in the Gaelic-speaking territory of the Decies will be "discovered" and soar to fame as one of the loveliest little harbours in these islands. Climbing its steep, bright, terraced streets with the rows of attractive houses one above the other in almost precipitous array, the visitor thinks of such fanciful foreign names as Sorrento, Tivoli or Marino.

But the tourist cannot be said to have seen Ardmore unless he follows its zigzag cliff street to its top most promenade - a pleasant grassy altitude. Here, if the visitor is favoured with a clear cloudless noon, the deep blue bay far below, with its wandering plateau of white sands, will suggest a superb sweep of French coast.

Yet Ardmore, true to its Gaelic name, is racy of the Irish sea and earth. Apart from the rich barley fields of East Munster that spread beyond the harbour to the upland horizon, and the soft verdure of the overhanging parks and gardens immediately beside you, Ardmore has memories and symbols of an Irish past that is hallowed and ageless. It has the roofless walls of as remarkable a medieval cathedral as will be found anywhere in the country. A few yards distant stands one of our ancient round towers, and close to the same group of buildings is the oratory, or Beannachan, which Rev. Professor Power reminds us is one of the earliest Christian structures surviving on Irish soil.

Indeed, one should not visit Ardmore without taking as guide a thorough and scholarly little work which Professor Power has written on its many shrines, wells and Ogham stones. The traveller will recall that striking symbolic sculpturing over the doorway of Notre Dame in Paris as he studies the time-worn panelling on Ardmore's twelfth century cathedral. Fortunately the same eminent priest-antiquarian of the Decies has interpreted for us those archaic mural carvings and drawings and their Biblical significance. Without such a key the symbolism might lose much of its meaning.

And again, the visitor should acquaint himself with the story and times of that great pre-Patrician missionary of this region - St. Declan, Patron of Ardmore. His influence seems still to dominate cliff and shore and is a living force in the life of the people. Love and legend too have kept fresh his memory along those summer sands.

It is thought that the little oratory marks the Saint's tomb. A relic - the head of St. Declan - was preserved at Ardmore until as late as the 17th century. And here is its subsequent story as it is set forth by Declan's learned biographer:

"The skull had become so worn and infirm from great age, much handling and long exposure, that in the year 1642 it had to be sent for repair to one Hercules Beer, silversmith, of Youghal. A history of Youghal written by Thomas Cooke, Clerk of that place, about the middle of the 18th century, and quoted by Hayman, is responsible for the story.

"Under the silversmith's hammer the head crumbled so to pieces that repair became impossible. Thereupon the dishonest silversmith substituted for the original relic the skull of one John Dromada, a felon, who a short time previously had suffered the extreme penalty of the law at Youghal. Upon the substituted skull Beer put a silver plate as if he had repaired it. The fraud was, however, soon detected, but in all probability not before it was too late to recover the original fragments."

I have an unforgettable memory of a road that runs eastward from Ardmore; it passes through the "Old Parish (believed to be the oldest parish in Ireland) and takes you across a broad highland moor of flowering heather. You are setting your face towards that country which was a fount of song for Geoffrey Keating and Donnchadh Ruadh MacConmara. Suddenly the sea, the sunset, and the massed mountains open out beneath you in a tremendous vision. Surely something mightier than ever artist painted or poet dreamed.

Partition cannot sever Ulster

Despite our economical, geographical and historical arguments, were Eire to lose those six counties of Ulster, the unseverable would still remain - the spiritual, the visionary, the indivisable national soul. And when this spirit is caught in poetry and literature it can outlast and challenge all artificial boundaries and divisions.

Thus the literary and poet voices of the now-partitioned Ulster challenge us out of the centuries and as long as those voices are heard the North-East of Eire can never be alien territory or foreign earth. When Columcille linked Derry in the North with Durrow in the Midlands and with Arran in the West, he was thinking of a common homeland - each suggested the fields and the fragrances of all Erin.

And it was on the shores of the now "alien" Six Counties his sad eyes rested as his exile coracle bore him away forever.

> *"From the plank of the oak where in sorrow I lie*
> *I am straining my sight through the water and wind*
> *And large is the tear of the soft grey eye*
> *Looking back on the land that it leaves behind".*

That land was the present "Six Counties", but to Columcille it was the shore of Eire. And lest there be any mistake, listen:

> *"To Erin alone is my memory given*
> *To Meath and to Munster my wild thoughts flow*
> *To the shores of Moy-linny, the slopes of Loch Leven,*
> *And the beautiful land the Ultonians know".*

Thus Ulster and the South, Leinster and Meath, Connaught and the West - each in all and all in each - the land of Ireland.

The name of Bangor in Co. Down will never suggest to the European scholar a distinct and foreign territory; he will think of Comgall and Columbanus and their very names will embody the old undivided land of Eire - the isle of learning - the Lamp of the West! So, too, when he recalls Emania and Ard Macha he will think of the whole earth of Ireland as surely as he will recall it again when he ponders on the names of Saul and Slemish and Downpatrick.

The literary past of the now partitioned Ulster suggests no note of racial distinction. On the contrary some of Ireland's best verses of national fervour have come out of that very land. The noblest lament for Thomas Davis came from the pen of one who was born in the hearty of unionist Belfast. Here is a stanza from the Protestant patriot, Sir Samuel Ferguson.

"I walked through Ballinderry in the springtime
When the bud was on the tree;
And I said, in every fresh-ploughed field beholding
The sowers striding free
Scattering broadcast forth the corn in golden plenty
On the quick seed-clasping soil,
Even such, this day among the fresh-stirred hearts of Erin,
Thomas Davis, is thy toil!"

And was it not Ferguson who sang so lyrically from the Gaelic in his "Fair Hills of Holy Ireland"?

And to show again that the spirit of a land when caught in the songs of here poets is indestructible and unbroken by boundaries one has but to recall the Belfast-born Eithne Carberry and Alice Milligan from the Tyrone hills. Even when "Moira O'Neill", who wrote "Songs of the Antrim Glens" was thinking of "Corrymeela and the low south wind", she had the mood and the raciness of all Ireland in mind.

What of partitioned Ulster's literature today and its relation to the rest of Ireland? In Belfast, again we have Cathal O'Byrne and Padraic Gregory steeped in the Gaelic tradition – authorities on Irish ballad and folk-song; nobody can set an Irish boundary to the overflowing wit of a George Shiels comedy or a play by Louis Walsh. Alice Milligan is true to the spirit of her earliest poems - the spirit of Irish unity. Indeed no other area of its size in the land fosters so many writers so Irish of the Irish as this North-East corner.

When we read Joseph Campbell's "Ploughing Song" the little fields of Armagh or Down are as homely to us as those of Clare or Wicklow or Galway, or wherever else our native surroundings are set.

Thus the literature of the Six Counties mingles with that of the Twenty-six and forges a heritage of the mind that can never be severed by Partition.

The Basket Maker

It was in the bog garden of the sallies that I first met him. I heard the merry whistling among the willows and though he carried a crutch and stick, his disabilities did not in the least affect his happy heart. The long green osiers newly cut lay on the pathway, and when I offered to carry them over to the house, he thanked me, but explained that the little lad who did this work for him would be disappointed. He would be here presently, and there was always a penny or twopence to be earned at the job.

The basket maker cultivated his own sallies: they flourished in long, green hedges in this garden of black, boggy earth. Tomorrow was the fair day at Glenaward, and the old man expected a complete sale.

He would not have it indeed but that I should go right up to the house with him to see the array of work that he was sending out to tomorrow's fair. Here surely was an exhibition in the sally-weaver's art. There were stout bread baskets; shopping baskets with neat handles; beautifully and delicately-worked flower baskets.

"Did you ever see a cliabh?" asked the rod-weaver looking with a smile of approval towards a great wicker-work container wrought in hazel. "Its not in many parts of Ireland they use them now", he added.

He showed me how it was hoisted on to the back. And I remembered then that in the West of Ireland two of these "cleeves" are balanced on a donkey's back when going to market. The same method is used in gathering home the turf or perhaps loads of seaweed from the strand. Then he had a number of wide, dish-like circular baskets. "For straining the potatoes for the dinner", commented the old man.

And then there were two other baskets that puzzled me; just for the moment I could not think of what uses they would be put to. One was a sort of cage for pigeons and the other was a trout basket.

"Though I'm an oul' man", says he "I always keep up to date". And he led the way to a little room off the kitchen. Here was his master-piece - a decorative wicker work table that would adorn the sitting room of any suburban villa. It was generous in size, durable and solid. It was woven throughout of daintily painted osiers and made peculiarly distinctive by bands of coloured sea-grass which were woven into the fabric.

He had many other useful and decorative articles in this sally and sea-grass effect; a cosy armchair was one. Who could guess that the green willow and the sea-grass could be fashioned into such things of beauty. "And Irish sea-grass, too", said the basket-maker with enthusiasm.

Bidding me make myself comfortable in the new armchair, he laid his work-knife aside and sat down on a low stool. Slowly teasing his tobacco and preparing his pipe, he gave me kindly pictures of his customers, far and near, in country and town. The man from Glasgow who came every summer to "the lake" always ordered trout-baskets for his friends. "Aye", said the sally-weaver with a little pride, "an the gintleman tells me the names o' the lakes where his friends fish .. far away from here. Loch Lomond and Loch Ness. There was a song whin I was a lad, 'The bonnie, bonnie banks o' Loch Lomond'. There's where some o' me trout-baskets go".

Then there was the little bird fancier from the town - he had been a sailor - but he always knew where to come for a good cage for a canary; the thrifty housewives from the Ulster border who were coming - many of them - with their menfolk to tomorrow's greatest market fair at Castleconnor. If only he could count all the dinner baskets and bread-baskets made from white peeled sallies that he had sold to the good housewives of Breffni. Mrs. O'Carroll (did I not know her, she kept prize poultry) - well, she had ordered the beautiful table. It was a wedding present for the newly married couple who had come to live in Ivy Lodge at McCarthy's Cross. The people who had rented the new bungalow in the village had ordered another table.

And so the basket-maker smoked contentedly, showing how his sally-weaving was the symbol of life itself. For over there at the far end of the room was the newly-woven cradle; and here was the old man's armchair, where tired age might sit after the stress and storm of the years.

Somebody told him that I was a "writing man", and he confessed that he read little beyond the local paper, yet he was glad to meet for the first time a man who wrote.

And here again I remembered that the rod-weaver's art is interwoven with that of the writer's, - for it is a basket, too, that is often the final receptacle of our early efforts and achievements - aye, the editor's waste-paper basket.

The Charm of Childhood

There is nothing in all literature quite so beautiful as a faithful and sympathetic portrayal of child life. I have been reading a book recently in which there are many touching pictures of childhood, the laughter and play, the simple games, the tears over broken dolls. The writer is Garrett O'Driscoll, a new Irish novelist whose first book "Noreen" (London:Roberts 7/6) is not only a work of promise but a decided achievement. It contains those original lyrical touches that are the sine qua non of good prose.

Those childhood pictures brought me back the half-forgotten gardens of my own youth - arcadian bowers rich with the scent of wet leaves and drowsy with the hum of bees. I remembered even the butterflies of childhood, the dragon-fly, fear-inspiring and beautiful; the moss upon old apple trees that have long since been destroyed and the exact spot in the meadow in which I used to hear the corncrake. The meadow itself came vividly back with its daisies and clover and celandines. The nook beside the lane in which I built a house of broken china and dreamed of the time when I would build a large house - aye, a castle or palace with turrets and towers and domes!

Happy time!

One is impressed too by the intense love for little children which finds expression in the songs of our greatest poets and in the novels of our foremost writers. Wordsworth, in his "Ode to Immortality" brings before us as only a great poet can, the paradise of childhood:

> *"Heaven lies about us in our infancy*
> *Behold the child among his new-born blisses*
> *Fretted by sallies of his mother's kisses*
> *With light upon him from his father's eyes!*
> *See, at his feet some little plan or chart,*
> *Some fragment from his dream of human life".*

Longfellow, Dickens, Robert Bridges - all have endeavoured to fathom the helplessness, the purity, the innocence of childhood. And we find such a beautiful thought in a translation from the Gaelic:

> *"I could not garner gold,*
> *The fame I found grew cold,*
> *With love came sorrows hold*
> *To blight my life's flower mild.*
>
> *I leave behind no fame,*
> *No glory and no shame,*
> *But, Oh, God! I would write my name*
> *Deep in the heart of a child".*

The "Wild Sweetness of Morning"

Childhood is all that is fresh, rich and wonderful.   It is the morning life and a summer's morning too.   The soul is in its baptismal innocence - a dawn flower born to bloom forever. The life of the daisy, of the violet, of the rose -   how brief it is, but this flower that is the soul of a child is destined for life immortal.   Before all flowers, all blossoms, all young life upon this earth the soul of a child is worthy of the best guardianship and care.

The Divine Invitation

"Suffer the little children to come to Me and forbid them not for of such is the Kingdom of Heaven".   In these words we have the Divine conception of childhood.   They are touching and terrible words -   touching insofar as this innocence is akin to the atmosphere of Paradise; terrible in the consequences of blighting such innocence.

The preserving of childhood's purity and innocence is one of the highest ideals towards which mankind could aspire.   "Blessed are the pure of heart for they shall see God".

To fathers and mothers the world over how many human lilies are entrusted - lilies more precious in God's sight than those flowers of the East that were more beautiful than the array of Solomon.

A Black Moment

The moment in which the soul of innocence is first sullied is a sad and a dark moment indeed for earth and heaven. Again, the Divine Lover of children warns him who would rob childhood of its innocence that it were better if a millstone were hanged about his neck and he were drowned in the depths of the sea.

The Future

The great saints of every age were once children and the mother who reads these words may hold on her knee at this moment the child who may yet become a world-known saint. How important it is that Catholic parents should fulfil to the letter their obligations towards their children..

"At Least You My Friends!" - *Some thoughts for November*

> *"These hearts were woven of human joys and cares,*
> *Washed marvellously with sorrow, swift to mirth,*
> *The years had given them kindness, dawn was theirs,*
> *And sunset and the colours of the earth."*

What Rupert Brooke wrote of the Flanders dead is true of all our deceased relatives and friends, whether they fell in battle, were cut down by disease, or were taken from us in any other of the thousand ways common to death.

When they were alive, we looked upon them as indispensable cogs in the cosmic machinery. Nay, we looked upon many of those neighbours and friends as essential to us in their sympathy, love and assistance. When some of them died, we felt that life for us had died with them, that the sun of joy had gone out, and the only future we could visualise was a vista of loneliness and emptiness. Psychologists must have noted, ere now, how prone are our minds to forget absent friends. New friendships, new environment, the affairs of today relegate to oblivion the faces and scenes and emotions of yesterday. Of course, there are exceptions to this rule, but they are few.

"The air is full of farewells to the dying", sings Longfellow. Full of farewells to the living, too. Step onto the platform of any of the big railway termini of our cities and look at the scenes of parting. Parental kisses, tear-dimmed eyes and silent handshakes, all testifying to the pain of saying farewell. But it is around the dying bed that we experience the grief that cannot be assuaged, the hoping against hope - the pang of sorrow that nothing, it seems, can ever appease. Only a few days pass sometimes, when grief is assuaged, appeasement comes and sorrow is healed. It is in the wise design of Providence that we do not break down utterly. But it is not in the Divine plan that our recovery from sorrow should mean that we are completely to forget the dead. Here is where human selfishness is to blame. "I was in prison and you did not come to me", Christ will say to the wicked at the last day.

Supposing that, for a political offence, a man was imprisoned and that the prison was next door to his own house, and suppose that he had been imprisoned for twenty years and that during that long term, none of his brothers or sisters next door went to see him, what would you think of them? "Cold! callous! selfish! inhuman! savage!" Yes, and that is what you and I are if we are forgetting the dead.

Five, ten, fifteen, or twenty years that once so dear friend of ours may be, perhaps, in the prison-house of Purgatory. How many times have we remembered him during that period? Maybe once or twice and then no more. And yet how we loved and laughed and played in the days gone by! He loved life as much as we did. When he was dying he asked us never to forget him in our prayers. We promised that we would remember him, and we sealed that promise with our tears! If we have broken trust, how are we to meet that dear face when our turn comes to pass through the dark portal?

It is the hope of the present writer that these reflections will engage the attention of the apathetic, for I fear there is too much apathy among us where the suffering souls are concerned. The doctrine of Purgatory should have a big place in our daily thoughts. Armistice days, cenotaphs, celebrations and church yard "patterns" have too much of the pomp of earth about them.. One simple heartfelt prayer is more efficacious than all of them together.

No day should pass without a prayer for our brothers and sisters in Purgatory. It is our duty, as members of the Church Militant, to help the Church Suffering. With our minds fully occupied by a round of engagements and amusements, life is at best an uncharitable and selfish affair. Do we realise that while we sleep and eat and drink and attend the theatres, our dear dead may perhaps be continually in pain - continually calling out to us from the depths of their anguish, "Have pity on us, have pity on us, at least you our friends!" Is not this a terrible truth? Shall we waken up to it now? In numerous ways we can help the Holy Souls. One simple ejaculation sent up fervently to God may open for one of them the gate of Heaven. Masses, Holy Communions, the forgoing of some little pleasure or amusement for their sake, are some of the most potent ways in which we can help.

Remembrance of the Holy Souls should enter largely into our daily lives - remembrance in the shape of a few short prayers. We should pray, not only for those we knew and loved, but for the great unknown and unseen who are suffering also.

In a little time the grass will be growing over us too, and the souls we have helped to heaven will pray for us. So let our resolution take shape in the immortal lines : "At the going down of the sun and in the morning we will remember them."

To Michael Walsh
(My Brother and childhood playmate)

Ah! have you gone, my poet-pal of childhood -
Gone without a murmur of adieu
To her who roamed with you thru Meath's green pastures,
While youth's unfolding pageant was yet new?

Our young hearts' yearnings we talked about together -
Ah! yes, God's glory always was your aim -
You whispered thus to me 'mid purpling heather:
"I long to tell the pagan of God's name."

In China's far-flung fields of ripening harvest,
As God's anointed you would labor there -
Ah! Michael, you were grieved the day He whispered
"Not thus, my son. Nor yet - not there, not there."

Your heart was sad, but yet with Faith intrepid -
God's glory still and Mary's your sole care -
And Patrick's and Columcille's and Brigid's -
You vowed that you would sing of them for e'er.

Nor yet did you forget fair Eire's charms -
God's gifts to her - the fairest land on earth,
Her fields of green, her slopes of sapphire stillness,
Her homely happiness around the old home hearth -

Her silent, silken lakes of shimmering silver,
Her rivulets half hidden in the glen,
Her rocks - her historied rocks - aye e'en the Mass Rock
All, all an honoured place found at your pen.

And now that you've obeyed the call eternal
Of Him, who long ago won your young love -
What songs - what sacred songs - are you now singing
With Eire's sainted son - Iona's dove?

And Mama - Michael - how did she receive you?
She left us - you remember - long ago.....?
Did you wake to see the same sweet smile of welcome...?
And - was she accompanied by James and Joe...?

Sister Mary Lucy Walsh
Sisters of the Holy Spirit
San Antonio - Texas, U.S.A.

Excerpt from Homily for Mass of Commemoration

15 June 1996 by V. Rev. Fr. Patrick Moore P.P.,
Parochial House, Kilbeg, Kells, Co. Meath, Eire.

The well lived sacrificial faith has brought vocations to the priesthood and religious life and has yielded up the gentle, poetic soul of Michael Walsh. All these saints, and Michael among them, are calling us together to draw worth and sustenance from his spiritual and poetic ideas, for our times. Surely this communion of saints is urging us to reflect on how he drank in the past and poeticised the depth, beauty, earthiness and charm of this place and of life itself. How could we pass by in such a milieu, his sensitivity to the natural, "summer meadows, the autumn fruit and grain touched with gold, the dewdrops and the last star and the moss green stepping stones of little streams." How could we not be unaffected by his family, his home, his landscape, his childhood, a touch of paradise revealed, in his first prayer with her - "who kissed me, joined my infant hands, and taught me how to pray," as she herself, his mother, "prayed on beads of brown." It cannot be other than the power and influence of the communion of saints that takes this into our vision and purpose now. Nor is it coincidental merely that Michael should be conscious of Oliver Plunket as he made reference in poetry to Loughcrew his birthplace, across the fields from here, or that he should have been the young man who helped Matt Talbot into the ambulance in a Dublin Street on that fatal day of his saintly life. There is a Providence that shapes our ends, come what may, and it is heavily evident in this great Communion of what, the late Monsignor Ronald Knox once called: "All saints, all souls and all sorts" which make up the Church travelling and arrived. Praise to God all you holy saints bringing us with a common purpose to work, reflect and pray today. Our gathering together this weekend will benefit many. It will enrich our minds with gentle ideas and grace our spirits with deep spiritual joy. But, above all, our worship and prayer with time and eternity bonded closely and deeply will draw us nearer our God or as Michael so aptly puts it; "SINCE IT IS PRAYER ALONE CAN ARCH THE INFINITE." We can be sure we are as close to God as Michael is and as he was in poetry and prayer on earth here as he prepared for paradise by way of Fore.

Michael Walsh
Some Personal Memories
By his Brother

It is fitting that I should record these few memories of my dear brother, Michael, for the IRISH CATHOLIC, for it was in the pages of the IRISH CATHOLIC that his first poem appeared well-nigh 25 years ago. The title of this little poem was "A Welcome to Summer." Pending the writing of a fuller biography I am concerned only in this brief memoir to indicate the influences which shaped him and made him what he was. Therefore, I am jotting down in chronological order, as they occur to me, the few outstanding features of his short life.

Childhood Scenes

He was born in an old whitewalled farmhouse on the slope of a hillside known as the Ben of Fore, or locally the Hill of Ben, in the heart of the beautiful lake-country of North Westmeath. The village of Fore, nestling at the foot of the Ben, was a famous seat of learning in ancient times, as testified by the many ruins of churches and monasteries, stone crosses and old city gates which remain to this day. From the summit of this hill above the house where he was born is visible the finest and most extensive view of beautiful landscape in all Westmeath. No fewer than five lakes can be seen within a radius of 20 miles all round. On a Summer day it is a magnificent sight to see from the hill-top those sparkling lakes, sprinkled all over the landscape, and shimmering in the sunlight. Little silver-bright rivers wind away from them in all directions through miles and miles of green countryside and brown bogland, broken here and there by clumps of rich woodland and low hills covered with yellow furze.

Even on the calmest day in Summer a gentle breeze plays around the hill-top, and the silence up there is only broken by the sudden buzz of a bee, as it rifles the heather-bells for honey. It was an ideal spot for a poet's birth-place, but it is comparatively little known to the outside world, as it is off the beaten track of the railways and the great trunk roads that link up the towns. Yet this enchanting countryside was the inspiration of most of his poems and essays. As he says himself in a chapter of his Autobiography published in *Bonaventura:*

"These still remain at the root of my poetry: the reeds in the bog, Summer coming in clouds of white daisies to the sloping fields at the back of the house, and the Hill of Ben itself like some Eternal Symbol amid the suns and mist of change," and in the same chapter he says: "From the half-door in daylight I could see the blue-grey outline of the Wicklow mountains; their faint dream-like distance allured. From my father's higher fields one could see that far-off entire range of mountains - calm with a seeming tranquillity that was not of this world." Such was the landscape of his childhood.

Parental Influence

His mother's early death, and the break-up of the family life which succeeded it, permanently saddened him, and is responsible for the note of melancholy which is a feature of many of his poems. He loved the old whitewalled house where he was born with a passionate intensity, and he recalled it lovingly years afterwards in a poem which appeared in the *Father Mathew Record:*

How well I know those walls
So happy in the dance
And flicker of the fire
Each miniature vale
On their uneven face
Each tiny rise and fall
And fissure in the stone
Each rafter, dark, uncouth,
The polished mantle beam,
The hearth's flat worn stones-
Here long ago for me
Eternity was born !
My infant up-turned face
All-wondering lost and deep
Within my mother's eyes
As holy word on word

110

Built up within my mind
The whole of earth and heaven
So simple were those words
That wrought first time for me
The image of my God !
How can this heart forget
How can it soon forget
Or evermore forget
Mean straw and stone and clay
But yet the door of all
That knows no shore in time
No bounds in any star !

From these lines it can be seen what a profound influence on his life was the religious instruction he had received from his much-loved mother. When he was a child, his father, who was a great lover of trees and flowers, used to carry Michael on his back around the fields at home, pointing out several trees he had planted years before, to the great joy of the coming poet. He never forgot those rambles through the meadows with his father, and it was to his father years later he dedicated his first book of poems, "Brown Earth and Green." Naturally, therefore the parental influence, combined with the charming countryside where he was born, turned his thoughts from "Nature up to Nature's God." Of course from his earliest years he read everything he could lay his hands on. He was fortunate on account of the fact that his grandfather was a great reader, and there were always plenty of books lying around Michael had a particular love for the poets, and early learned to appreciate the beauty of the "lyric line."

But now I must pass over some years, and tell of the next great influence that came into his life. I refer to his meeting with Father Joseph McDonnell, S.J., who was the saintly Editor of the *Irish Messenger of the Sacred Heart* for 25 years until his death in 1928.

Father McDonnell, S.J.

A poem of Michael's (I forget the name of it now), appeared in the *Connacht Tribune,* and attracted the attention of Fr. McDonnell who immediately got in touch with the young writer. The result of this meeting was that Michael began to write poems for the *Messenger*. Fr. McDonnell, after the manner of the patrons of old, fostered and developed the writing powers of his young protege, and helped to lay the foundation of that individual method of writing which critics of his later work have styled "charming."

For 20 years he continued to write articles and poems for the *Messenger*, whose wide circulation made his name known in many homes in Ireland and beyond the seas. His poems were all of an intensely devotional character, simply written, in accordance with the wishes of his Editor, who himself, in Biblical phrase, combined the wisdom of the serpent with the simplicity of the dove. When Fr. McDonnell had known Michael for some years, he suggested to him that, perhaps, he would like to study for the priesthood. Michael was overjoyed at the suggestion, and confessed that he cherished the same desire himself, in secret, but there were many obstacles in the way: The kindly priest helped Michael to sweep away the obstacles, with the result that shortly afterwards he began his studies in the Apostolic School, Mungret. He studied so hard there, and later on at St. Finian's, Mullingar, that he overtaxed his strength and his health broke down. This was a heart-breaking blow to him, but Fr. McDonnell was at hand to console him. He suggested that this breakdown in Michael's health meant that it was not his vocation to be a priest, but that his aptitude for writing so well on devotional subjects fitted him to become a Catholic journalist, and do good by his writings. Michael never forgot this advice of his friend and counsellor, and acted upon it to his dying day. And as Fr. McDonnell predicted, he did do good by this form of Catholic Action, for his pen always mirrored his thoughts, and I have in my possession a letter from a young Irish nun in America telling me she was inspired to give her life to God after reading a poem of Michael's in the *Messenger* entitled "The Nun."

When Michael recovered his health somewhat, Father McDonnell offered him a post in the *Messenger* Office and he continued to write for the *Messenger* month after month under the wise guidance of its Editor. Time passed, and Father McDonnell after a long life spent in doing good, was called to his reward, and Michael lost his best friend and adviser. By this time he had left the *Messenger* Office and was earning his living by free-lance journalism. He loved to write for all the religious periodicals in Ireland, and it was impossible to pick up most of them for some years before his death without coming across his name at the foot of an article or poem. After Father McDonnell's death he still continued to write for the *Messenger* under subsequent Editors, his work finding favour with such men as Father T. Ryan, S.J., now in China; Father Jerome Mahony, S.J., and the present Reverend Editor, Father Scantlebury, S.J. He also wrote for the *Irish Monthly, Irish Rosary, The Cross, The Irish Catholic, The Standard* and *The Far East*.

Happy Family Life

Rev. Fr. Senan, O.M. Cap., Editor of the *Father Mathew Record*, and Rev. Fr. Jerome, O.F.M., Editor of *Assisi*, appreciated his work particularly, as they recognised its intrinsic integrity, and the genuine faith from which it sprang. He also wrote for the *Leader, Cork Examiner, Westmeath Examiner*, and the two Dublin Dailies, *Irish Press and Irish Independent*. It was about this time he became acquainted with the lady who afterwards became his wife. She was a Wexford school teacher and also a writer; and Michael and she were married after a short engagement and settled down to twelve years of domestic happiness in a quiet part of County Wexford, near Cullenstown School, where his wife taught. During all this time he wrote incessantly. He was not without his trials, ill-health, etc., which is the common lot of all families, but through it all he remained bright and cheerful. He had a great sense of humour and no one enjoyed a good joke better than what he did. He was very happy in his married life as he and his wife were ideally matched. Their books and one or two personal friends, including a priest, made happiness for them. The Catholic religion in all its aspects was very often discussed between this group around the fire. They were blessed with a large family whom they cherished and brought up in the true Irish Catholic tradition. The family Rosary was never omitted. It was not known until after his death that he used to give alms regularly out of his scanty means. Then some poor people whom none of his family knew came to mourn him and told of his kindness to them when living.

As Fr. Stephen Brown, S.J. finely said, "All of us live a two-fold life, an outward and an inward. The latter may be feeble in some, intense in others." The inward life was intense in Michael; in fact, he could be called a mystic, in the sense that he was always conscious of the presence of God, and the next world was as real to him as this one. Therefore, it is not surprising to learn that he was familiar with the thoughts and writings of the great mystics of the Church like St. Teresa, St. John of the Cross, St. Catherine of Genoa, and St. Catherine of Siena.

His Last Illness

During his last illness he was nursed very devotedly by the kind Sisters of St John of God in the Haughton Hospital, New Ross. The four nuns, Mother Malachy, Sister Rena, Sister Frances and Sister Vogue, who took care of him, were much edified by his constant prayers. Even in the delirium of pneumonia he made the responses to the Litany most fervently, praying with all his failing strength. Later, on the instructions of the Doctor in charge, he was removed to a nursing home in Waterford. The nursing brothers who received him here told members of his family afterwards that he was not long under their care until word went forth through the community of a hundred Brothers, that they were nursing "a man of God." On taking leave of his dear wife for the last time, he said to her "The breath of Paradise is beautiful." Brother Edmund Campion was present at the end. He relates; "Michael had lain quietly for some hours without speaking, and then I raised him on pillows in a reclining position to assist his breathing, as the end approached. He thanked me, and shortly afterwards his head drooped sideways on the pillow, and he went out like a light." It was three o'clock in the afternoon of Thursday, December 1, 1938. He was 41 years old when he died, but when his body was laid out after death he looked like a young man of 28. His features were set in a happy smile, and he seemed to be only in a calm and peaceful sleep. All the colour had not gone from his face even when the coffin lid was being screwed down. It was night when the coffin was borne out to the waiting hearse, escorted by the priest and acolytes between two long rows of Brothers with lighted candles, chanting the hymn "In Paradisum." It was just the beautiful religious pageantry he would have loved to write about. The Brothers carried his coffin down the massive stone steps of the monastery and placed it in the hearse, and as the flickering candles grouped themselves together around the scene the cold December stars shone out above them in the night-blue darkness. Then the hearse began the long journey to Wexford, to lay his body in the church where he was married twelve years before.

It was the early sunset of a calm December evening as I sadly followed his coffin through the streets of Wexford and across the long bridge over the beautiful Slaney to the quiet cemetery of St. Ibar. The landscape of his adoption was draped in an unearthly beauty. The sky was clear and cold except in the west, where a group of silver clouds were clustered round the setting sun, and woodland and river lay still in the evening light. It was then the last verse of one of his last poems came back to me:

"Oh! God, when weary with the days
And evening skies are over me
By ships of cloud and sunset bays
May I at last go home to Thee".

In Memoriam

(To my dear brother, Michael Walsh).

You sang of Patrick, on the slopes of Slemish,
Tending his flock, beneath a Winter sky,
And lifting up his voice in supplication,
A hundred times a day, to the Most High.

You sang of Brigid, maid of heavenly beauty -
Whose every thought and action was a prayer -
About her snowy feet the young lambs playing,
In the starry meadows of her own Kildare.

You sang of Columcille, a lonely exile,
Dreaming of Durrow on dim Iona's shore,
Your tears were mingled in your yearning
For your lost home beside the Ben of Fore.

But now you've found those saints you cherished
From your young years to manhood's golden prime
Holding the Heavenly Portals wide to greet you,
As to Eternity you passed from time.

And Patrick, on his child, bestows his blessing,
And Brigid smiling, bids her lover "Come!"
And Columcille, the exile of Iona,
Welcomes a brother exile Home.

Memories In An Old Schoolhouse

The very first thing I learned at school - with the help of liberal applications of the cane - was how to read the clock.

My old schoolmaster, for whom I had a wholesome respect, but no love, was a near relative.

I used to harbour an uneasy suspicion, sometimes amounting to certainty, that whenever punishment with the cane was indicated for me, he did not err on the side of leniency in order to demonstrate to the other pupils that no exception was being made on the score of mere relationship. In later life, when he retired from teaching and I could speak to him on equal terms, I found him a most charming man.

What Time Is It?

I was sent to school at three years old, and my relative had a most disconcerting habit of turning to me suddenly in the middle of a lesson with what seemed to be a wholly irrelevant question, "What time is it?". I would stare blankly at the mysterious figures on the dial of the big school clock, high up on the wall near the fireplace, as if in a mute appeal to reveal its secrets to me. But all in vain.

The cane was produced once more, and with the palms of my hands still sore, the master would make another attempt to explain the very intricate functions of the hour and the minute hand to me. But it was a red-letter day for me when at last I learned to read the clock correctly, and I still remember the glow of achievement, the sense of mastery, that came over me when I had solved this first difficult problem of my life.

A Museum Piece

One's schooldays, whether happy or unhappy, remain in the memory for ever, and so when the present teacher invited me, on a recent visit, to come in and see my old school, I was grateful for the opportunity. The self-same clock that had cost me so many slaps was there still, but no longer a mystery.

What childhood memories came back to me again as I contemplated the long yellow pine desks where I used to sit, now scored like Ogham stones with the furtive pen-knives of generations of schoolboys. In the floor I saw once more the two semi-circles of worn brass studs where countless young feet "toed the line" in the classes of long ago.

And there, hanging on the far wall, was the big map of the world, now yellow and faded, and dim as a dream, I remembered being once slapped for not knowing the whereabouts of the Comoro Islands on this map, and I began to search for them again, but they eluded me once more. A legend printed in black at the bottom of the map still informed all and sundry that "British possessions are coloured red", but the red had vanished with the years, leaving no trace.

Two world wars have come and gone since the map was printed, rendering the names of many cities and countries obsolete, and I fancy it is now retained only as a museum piece.

Sacks In The Kiln

Everywhere my eyes wandered evoked a memory. Looking out through the front windows, the magnificent panorama of my childhood rose up before me once again: two mighty prehistoric forts, rising one above the other from their green earthen enclosure, and behind them again, rising higher still like the painted scenery at the back of a stage, the massive upland ridges, bright with yellow flowering furze, and stretching from Farrell's Hill to the summit of the Ben of Fore.

Out in the playground, while waiting for the master to arrive in the morning, there used to be a game played called "Sacks in the Kiln". Two or three of the bigger fellows would chase and capture the smaller ones and pile them on the grass in a pyramid calling out at the same time "Sacks in the Kiln; any more coming in?" as each youngster in turn was thrown on the pile. I well remember the feeling of being half-smothered, when I happened to be the under "sack" with eight or nine others piled on top of me.

Reading the Paper

But a hush would fall on the noisy crowd when the master was seen approaching in the distance. He was always very punctual, and "Good morning, boys", was his invariable greeting as he turned the key unlocking the big school door. In his pocket he always carried the daily newspaper - at that time it was the "Freeman's Journal" - to be carefully unfolded and read at lunch-time.

Normally, he used to read his paper in silence, but sometimes the news would be too exciting to keep to himself. I remember when the King of Portugal was assassinated by an anarchist, he explained to us what anarchy meant, as well as the whole history of Portugal. To be able to distinguish what was first-rate from what was not, he used to tell us, was the mark of an educated man. He used often give me the newspaper in the evening to take home to my grandfather, who in his turn would pass it on to Old Maura, a very remarkable old neighbour who lived further down the valley.

The Shepherd's Wife

It was through my friendship with Old Maura that I really learned to love reading for its own sake. I used to go down to her with the newspaper on a Sunday evening, just when the night was closing in, and the shadows were gathering round the Ben. A dignified, gentle, grey-haired old woman, with a fresh complexion that belied her eighty years.

She had been a governess in her youth with some rich family, and had travelled the world. Then she settled down late in life, and was married to a simple, honest, old country man, a bearded shepherd who spoke but seldom, and spent most of his time looking after stray sheep on the heathery slopes of the Ben.

There was no family, and her husband did not share her taste for reading, but they lived a quiet Darby and Joan existence in the evening of their days. She was very hospitable, and I remember, once in the lambing season, she gave me, as a great treat, tea flavoured with goat's milk, together with hot buttered pancakes made on sheep's milk, which tasted delicious. Their cosy house nestled at the foot of the hill, which rose in a steep slope above it. A few white pigeons, roosting up in the smoky rafters, kept them company at night.

Old Maura used to sit down in a big armchair in the chimney corner, when her household work was done, with a bright turf fire burning on the hearth.

The Night And The Day

On the wall behind her chair hung the lamp, with its clear glass globe and shining tin reflector - which she lit at nightfall. Near the lamp, also, were hung two pairs of well-worn brown Rosary beads, with big brass crosses. Beside her chair, too, was a vast and cavernous cupboard, filled to overflowing with old periodicals, magazines and books. She appeared to have an inexhaustible store, from which I gathered my weekly ration of reading matter every Sunday night and though it was never replenished, like the widow's cruse of oil in the Scripture, it never ran dry.

She talked far into the night, and her voice was soft and low, for she had studied elocution and poetry in her youth, and loved a literary turn of phrase. I remember saying to her once that she must be lonely for lack of visitors (I believe I was her only one) and she answered me simply by saying: "My visitors are the night and the day".

She would talk to me of books far into the night, and during the pauses in the conversation, I could hear the homely chirp of a cricket in the hob, or the occasional soft flutter of a pigeon's wings stretching and preening itself among the shadows in the rafters. And then she would continue to tell of all the friends she knew in the past, from countesses to maid-servants, and of the few who were married and the many who were dead, and there I would sit listening to her in calm content while the fire burned low, and the hands of the clock stole softly round to the Rosary hour, while she continued to review the bygone scene, and "summon from the shadowy past the forms that once had been".

Boyhood in a Quiet Valley

Yellow furze and white hawthorn blossomed on the banks on each side of the long boreen leading to my childhood home.

Primroses starred the bottom of the ditches.

It was really a very quiet and forgotten valley between two hills and yet I never remember being lonely, even though I often saw nobody except the members of my own family from one Sunday to another. It was a place to dream in, and to imagine all the wonderful things that would come my way when I would grow up and go out into the big world beyond the hills.

Books and dreams were the substance of my childhood, and I was never lonely, but many a wandering visitor used to come down the long laneway from the red gate to break the even rhythm of the days.

The Look of a Pirate

Out of the many I remember the few. There was "Old Nicholas," a bald and venerable rascal with an impressive beard like an Old Testament prophet, whom I once heard my father address as "Sir," so great was his natural dignity. He used to wear a huge red handkerchief knotted like a scarf round his neck, giving him the look of a pirate. To think of him as begging would be an outrage, rather he seemed to be conferring a favour, as he poked in his head over the half-door with the request, "I ask your leave to sleep in the barn to-night."

He would come towards evening carrying over his shoulder a little bag of potatoes. From his belt hung a smaller bag of oaten meal, all of which he collected from friends and well-wishers whom he honoured with a visit. This was the invariable alms given to the poor man or woman who travelled the roads of Westmeath in my youth - potatoes and oaten meal - never money. In any case money was scarce, but food was plentiful.

I used to gaze with fascination at "Old Nicholas" on his monthly visit. Politely he would request my mother to let him have the use of a pot to boil some potatoes for his supper. She would make conversation such as "Well, Nicholas, any news on your travels"? "Nothin' worth bleatin," he would reply and lapse into silence again.

A Bed in the Barn

When the potatoes were boiled, they would be turned out into a round wicker basket, the hot water falling into a pot underneath. Then he would request a noggin of buttermilk with some salt and pepper. The amount of potatoes he required for his supper never failed to astonish me. Nothing was ever left in the basket but a huge heap of skins when "Old Nicholas" had finished. Then he would light his pipe and make his way to the barn which was situated a little distance from the house.

There was usually a pile of straw there from the previous harvest, and a few empty sacks lying around. My father would shake up the straw, and spread the empty sacks over it to make a rough but comfortable bed. "Old Nicholas" always slept in his clothes, and after warning him to be careful when lighting his pipe so as not to set fire to the straw, my father would bid him "Good-night" and close the barn door.

Next morning he would re-appear in the kitchen again, where my mother would provide him with a bowl of stirabout and fresh milk before sending him on his way. On his departure, he never failed to wish us all "health, wealth and prosperity."

Sale by Intimidation

Then there was the "tay man." A truculent fellow with a waxed moustache, high white starched collar and cuffs, and wearing an impressive gold chain across his waistcoat, he use to come driving down the boreen in a dashing high trap, drawn by a young and spirited horse. His method of salesmanship could be summed up in one word, "intimidation."

122

My mother was gentle and somewhat timid, and she would try to tell him she did not want his tea, as she always bought from the the local grocer in Fore, whose tea was famous in the parish. But this did not deter "your man". He would launch out into a long eulogy of his particular brand of tea, and make her feel almost a criminal for daring to prefer any other tea to his.

During this long tirade of abuse he held the driving whip in his hand and looking back on the incident, I verily believe that she was half afraid of him, for, when he insisted on leaving a sample half-pound of tea for a trial, even though it cost more, she took it meekly to get rid of him.

Barefooted Liberty

In the long Summer days we used to go barefooted and I remember my school fellows would ask one another: "When will your mother let you go barefooted?" It was a real treat to get rid of our heavy nailed boots at the first touch of Summer and to feel the cool grass under our feet once again. We gambolled about in the pastures barefooted, like young calves let our for the first time, until we got used to the new sensation of freedom.

Of course there was always the risk of getting a thorn in the foot or a stonebruise, but the sense of barefooted liberty was worth it all. Washing out feet every night before going to bed was an ordeal for most of us, but it was sternly insisted on by our parents.

And this reminds me of the most important travellers of all who ever came to our door, with bare feet and sandals, in the days when I was young.

Search for a Blessing

Brown habited, tonsured, clean-shaven men of God they were, from the great abbey at Multyfarnham. What a thrill it was for me the first time I saw them come on their questing journey. Two of them came down the boreen on a side-car driven by a stranger from miles away. I remember vividly the deep impression of sanctity left on my childish mind, as the first tall sandalled friar entered the house, and my mother knelt for his blessing.

In the Summer time they used to come when I was barefooted, and I would solemnly consider the incredible whiteness of their feet. Their clean, closely cut toenails beneath the brown habit fascinated me. It was as if the large statue of Saint Anthony in my mother's bedroom has suddenly come to life.

My father was away at the mill the first time they came and when he returned in the evening my mother said to him, "The friars from Multy were here and left their blessing for you."

"Thanks be to God," said my father. "Oh, they are the great men."

I was very young, and somewhat puzzled over the blessing being left, as I thought it was something tangible like a holy medal, and I remember searching behind the blue plates on the dresser, where my mother kept her letters and trinkets, but I failed to find the blessing. Looking back on it all now:

> *"I know 'twas childish ignorance*
> *But yet its little joy*
> *To know I'm farther off from Heaven*
> *Than when I was a boy."*

Memories of the Midlands

The yellow black-lettered poster had been up for weeks. Pasted with grimy fingers against old walls and trees along the roadside, they announced the coming of the first travelling cinema show to the village.

Hitherto announcements of fairs, auctions of new and old meadow hay, with perhaps an occasional political meeting thrown in, had monopolised local attention. But here was something really new, something never seen before, something not to be missed.

The village itself was a little triangle of roadside houses, hidden away in a fold of the green Midland hills. A roughly carved ancient stone cross stood in the centre of the green like a strayed spectator from another age. Near this the long barn-like canvas tent was being erected.

Not Allowed Go

How well I remember the first night it opened, for my father said I was far too young to be allowed to go, that I would be "walked on". So I lingered outside, envying all the lucky grown-ups filing in one by one.

After a while the sound of loud laughter from inside the tent drove me wild. I too wanted to see the new wonder, and after vainly trying to get a glimpse of the screen when the flap-door of the tent opened and shut, I wandered around in the darkness towards the back, and eventually spotted a small hole high up in the canvas wall.

There was an empty barrel standing nearby on which I climbed. I managed to enlarge the hold a little by poking a tiny finger through it at various angles, trying to stretch the untearable canvas. I remembered a broken penknife in my pocket, but my conscience baulked at doing too much damage.

However, with perservance I got the opening large enough to see clearly with one eye. The whole screen was just visible at an oblique angle and all would have been well had I kept quiet. But there was one scene shown in which the clown tripped over the ropes of a rising balloon and was lifted up bodily, arms and legs dangling in the air.

Taken From Perch

It was so funny that I broke out into a loud laugh, completely forgetting the necessity of silence. Shortly afterwards a big strong hand thrust up through the darkness from behind hauled me down off my perch.

One of the proprietor's minions had heard my illicit laughter and came round to investigate. Thus ended ingloriously my first cinema show. Many another picture I have seen since then from the comfortable plush seats of the modern cinema, but I do not think I ever laughed so whole-heartedly again as I did at that first stolen glimpse of the screen.

Another epoch-making event in my childhood was the coming of the motor-car during the first decade of this century. It was a sunny day in Spring, and a few other youngsters and myself were helping a neighbouring farmer to sow potatoes in a high field on the slopes of the only eminence of note in the district.

Far below us the little narrow dusty road ran through the valley. Suddenly the hired man cried out: "Oh, lads took down, quick! Do you see the big cloud of dust rolling down the road. That must be a motor car".

Horseless Carriage!

We all looked down and saw dimly a mysterious object tearing along the road at the speed of a railway train, half-hidden in the dust from its flying wheels. This was our first sight of the new invention everyone was talking about, the fulfilment of Saint Colmcille's prophecy that "carriages without horses shall go".

The first motor car had come to our valley; the age of speed had arrived, and the children playing on the roads would never play in safety again. Thereafter until we got used to it we would leave our work in the fields when the sound of a motor was heard in the distance and hasten to the roadside to watch it go by.

This radio is such a commonplace now that it is hard to realise that it also is comparatively new, but I must record its first impact on our quiet valley. The crystal set had just given way to the loudspeaker, and the Garda Barracks in the nearest market town had installed the first one.

Everyone from far and near came to hear it until the novelty had worn off. Even an eighty-year-old man went to hear it when a lecture happened to be broadcast from "2 RN".

Few Planes Still

The coming of the aeroplane has not made much difference to the lives of the people in the valley, as this particular part of the Midlands is far away from the recognised air routes, and the sound of an aeroplane is rarely heard even today.

On a recent visit to this enchanting country of my youth I found the rural electricity scheme making great strides. But here and there is still to be found a sturdy old-timer who will have nothing to do with "the new light". His invariable reply to the repeated requests of the canvassers is: "You can wire me up if you like, but you will get no money".

Vocation

"Leave all and follow me"-
She shrinks away in fear,
(The still, small Voice within her
She has not heart to hear)
For human love she must forego
At the Whisper in her ear.

And now she hears another voice,
"Lovers will come to woo,
And one you'll choose among them all
To give your heart unto;
Then down the years, until the end
Life will be sweet to you."

The first Voice whispers once again:
"Yes, Love is all your due,
You're fair and young and beautiful
But I am calling you
To sacrifice these gifts to Me,
And trust Me to be true.

"For I alone am ever true-
The Lord of Heaven above-
And now that I have chosen you
Leave all, and come, My dove,
Give Me your heart, I'm jealous, too,
And brook no other love.

"When emptied of each earthly wish
You've hearkened to My call,
And cast away the human love
That bars Mine like a wall,
I'll fill your soul with heavenly joy
When you have given Me all!"

She's vanquished now, and weeping, prays
For courage strong to take the sword

That cuts all earthly joy away.
"My only Love! My God adored!
O strengthen me! Thou art my All!
Behold the handmaid of the Lord!"

The Road to Damascus

When Paul west down Damascus way,
The Christians there, in chains to bind,
A shining cloud shut out the day,
And he was stricken blind.

A heavenly Voice spoke from the cloud,
In accents sweet, the Holy Name,
Paul, hearing, wept and sorrowed loud,
His heart with sudden love aflame.

We go our way, we sinners all,
Each walks his own Damascus Road,
Each hears the Voice that spoke to Paul,
The Voice of an offended God.

For deep within us - as a well -
Where Conscience reigns, serene, apart,
We hear His Voice, a warning bell,
In secret cloisters of the heart.

Oh, may we always heed His call,
May we be filled with sorrow true,
And cry aloud to Him with Paul,
"Lord, what will You that I should do".

Homeward in the Spring

When the time came for me in my teens to leave the green and airy hillside fields where I was born, to look for a job in the city, there was a family council.

"Your poor grandfather insisted on having you called after Uncle William when you were christened," said my father reproachfully, "in the hope that he'd make a priest out of you." Though it was the first time I had heard of such a laudable intention, I looked suitably contrite, for the implication was that I had somehow failed both grandfather and Uncle William. Now, the usual thing in the country is to have the eldest son called after the grandfather, but the dear old man had waived his claim in my case, in the hope that Uncle William might help to make his dream for me come true.

A word about Uncle William: "a man severe he was and stern to view," a bachelor schoolmaster lamed by an accident in early life, so that he always walked with the aid of a stick. Being unmarried, he was reputed to have money. His affliction may have soured him somewhat, but in any case he never took much notice of me, and I certainly was not the favourite among his vast army of nieces and nephews.

Though spasmodically pious, I am afraid I never possessed the staying power that is implied by an ecclesiastical vocation. Uncle William's keen old eyes, accustomed for many long years to size up the aptitudes of countless schoolboys, must have noticed all along that his nephew did not quite measure up to grandfather's ideal, for he never even suggested the possibility of a vocation to me. Of course, had I known what was intended, I might have tried to be different, but now, alas, it was too late, and Uncle William's money would never be wasted in trying to make a priest out of such unpromising material.

So, little man, what now? Somebody suggested a shopboy, a name that has long since gone out of fashion. But then it connoted what is known now as a white-collar job. I was not too keen on it, but there was not much choice.

Anything, however, to take me away from work on the land, and from my father's continual assurances that I was utterly useless to him. Just then a mutual friend heard of a Dublin publican who needed an apprentice.

It was a soft mild morning in early Spring, and the missel thrush was singing outside my window, when my father yoked old Bob to the cart, to drive both of us the six-mile journey to Oldcastle station to catch the early train for Dublin. It was the first time I had ever been in a train, but having read all about trains long before, I soon felt quite at home travelling through the lovely fields of Meath, now greening with the approach of Spring.

My new boss was a big man with a stern face, cold ruthless eyes, and heavy pointed moustache like Lord Kitchener, whose portrait I remembered from the Boer War.

Such a lot of signing of papers on behalf of my father and myself followed - indentures with red wafer seals attached - until I really began to feel I was being enlisted for life. All I remember of the difficult legal jargon was that in consideration of spending three years' apprenticeship indoor without a penny, Kitchener would guarantee to teach me my craft, and my father was to keep me in pocket money.

Those were the days when the public-houses opened at 7 or 8 in the morning and did not close till nearly midnight. So there I was, a raw apron-clad country youth starting my new career by learning the difference between a pint of plain and a pint of stout, and how to pull the black liquid through the pumps successfully together with the proper angle at which to hold the glass, so as to ensure the requisite creamy head to please the customer.

At that time the bulk of the customers were a noisy mob of British soldiers from a near-by barracks, Ship Street, I think. They were the Buffs, just returned from India, and bronzed with the Indian sun. Resplendent in their scarlet tunics with buff cuffs and facings, they made the somewhat dingy pub look gay and colourful as they thronged in night after night. They were friendly enough fellows if not too choice in their language. Their invariable drink was a bottle of Bass, which they always pronounced "Boss."

There were no stream-lined or chromium-plated pubs in those days in Dublin. Among a varied selection of customers, there was always the chancer ready to take advantage of the new apprentice, drinking a few big gulps out of his glass of plain, and then asking to have it topped up again with stout, as if it were the most natural thing in the world to do, and even making you feel that it was an honour to oblige him.

After some weeks I was getting quite accustomed to the routine, and seemed to have found favour with the boss, until something happened. A ne'er-do-well who used to go to school with me, and who left the country for the country's good long before, blew in one day and discovered me behind the counter. Unluckily he made a habit of coming in every day after that. He meant well, of course, but he always managed to call to talk to me when the boss was there. I don't know what the boss thought, but I could see he did not like it.

Torn between the wish not to appear cold to an old school friend, and still to mind my job. I had not the courage to tell him that he was making my position precarious.

He offered to show me the town, and I was glad enough of his company on my free afternoon weekly, but it just happened that in his zeal to show me new places he kept me out too late one night. It was just the opportunity that the boss was waiting for. I was due in at ten o'clock, but it was a quarter past when I arrived, and the door to my room was locked. I had to ring, and Kitchener opened the door himself.

He gave me a black look and said "I'll see you in the morning." Immediately after breakfast he saw me. "Have you your fare home?" he demanded. I had exactly five shillings pocket money, and the fare would be four-and-sixpence. "Yes," I said. "Well, you can go now," he said, "you don't suit me at all," and waited to see me out of the side-door.

I did not want to go home, having the neighbours say I was a failure. I could already imagine some of their comments, "He went to Dublin to see what o'clock it was and now he's back," and such-like sarcasms. I looked up the "situations vacant" in that day's papers, only to find when I went after them that they were already filled or at least that is what they told me.

I wandered into a couple of the city churches to say a prayer for a job, so that I might not have to go home again, but the doors of Heaven were of brass, and would not open. I was too young then to realise that some prayers are wisely left unanswered. I had eaten nothing all day since breakfast, and now it was evening and I was very hungry. The Oldcastle train was due to pull out about six o'clock.

Then I decided at last to spend my precious sixpence. I bought a supply of currant buns and some biscuits for fivepence, and for the other penny I bought two different halfpenny newspapers. "Now," said I to myself, "I have food for both body and mind until I get home."

As I settled myself back in the corner of the third-class carriage with two and a half hours train journey before me, and my unread newspapers on the seat beside me, I thought how a love of reading was a cushion against nearly all misfortunes. I could lose myself in these newspapers, and forget, temporarily at least, all my troubles.

Besides, now that defeat was inevitable why not sit back and enjoy it. I had read somewhere in Homer, I think, "The gods do not mind defeat" so I was in good company.

So the long slow journey passed pleasantly enough between my newspapers and my thoughts. But the enjoyment ceased at Oldcastle, the terminus of the line, when I was decanted out into the darkness, with a six-mile walk between me and my home. However, my good spirits returned at the Weasel's Corner, for the moon came out over the cairn-topped hills of Loughcrew and brightened the road ahead.

A fox barked in the woods of Glannaward and the vixen answered him back from the rock of Carrick. A waterhen fluttered in a roadside pond and a solitary snipe drummed and circled overhead. There was no other sound except the ringing out of my footsteps on the hard dry road, and the peace of the calm Spring night drenched in moonlight, began to sink into my soul. Presently in the distance I could distinguish that land mark of my heart, the shadowy outline of the Ben of Fore greeting me like an old friend.

There it was, waiting for me to return from the hard pavements of the city, back to its sheltering slopes again where I was born. It was midnight when I arrived home, and I felt it was too late to disturb my father. He was a light sleeper, and the lifting of the latch would have wakened him. Besides, I did not feel equal to any explanation that night of my sudden return.

Then I remembered the barn. There would be sweet fragrant sheaves of straw there, and many a wayfarer had slept there often before me. In any case, I needed time to collect my thoughts.

I was grateful for the warm comfort of the barn, for the familiar sound of old Bob champing in his stable next door, and the quiet breathing of the cattle chewing their cud in the darkness of the cowshed across the yard. It had been a strenuous day, much had happened since old Kitchener had fired me that morning, the long, aimless walking through unfriendly city streets; the fruitless attempts to get another job, the unanswered prayers.

Suddenly I was very tired, and nothing in the whole wide world was so lovely and desirable at that moment as sleep - long, sweet sleep. "Yes, to-morrow," I murmured to myself as I snuggled deeper and deeper into the warm, sweet-smelling yellow straw, "to-morrow, I'll tell my father - everything - everything - but now I must sleep."

Spring in the Midlands

Our little farm sprawled - a patchwork quilt of green and brown
fields - across the massive shoulder of the Ben.

The Ben of Fore would be regarded as a very modest hill among
the heather-clad giants of Wicklow, but it was a veritable mountain
in the midlands where the miles of brown bog stretched away to
the foot of the Slieve Blooms.

I recall a Spring scene of fifty years ago in the airy upland fields.
Bob, our old black horse, is yoked to a cart by the barn-door, and
my grandfather is eyeing the mackerel sky doubtfully, for the
weather is all important on this day of Spring sowing.

To the Upland Field

"It is getting bright at the butt of the wind" he calls to my father,
who is just emerging from the barn with a heavy sack of oats upon
his shoulder. "If you can see a patch of blue sky the width of a
sailor's jacket, we'll have a fine day".

My father looks up and shakes his head. He has no time for my
grandfather's picturesque phrases. He silently loads the sack of
oats on the cart and taking Bob by the winkers, leads him up the
stony path to the Bush Hill, an upland field which took its name
from a lonesome bush growing in the centre, beneath which
bloomed the first primrose of the Spring.

My grandfather is tying together two corners of a strong white
linen sheet to sling it around his neck like a huge pinafore.
Gathering up the folds on his arm he follows my father. The
sloping field is freshly ploughed and the sack of gleaming white
oats is opened on the headland. My father scoops out the heavy
grain with his two hands into the old man's apron, who is firmly
convinced that no member of the family can sow the seed like
himself.

"That's enough" said my grandfather. "I am not as young as I used to be", and gathering up the folds of the sheet in his left hand, he straightens himself up like a soldier, with his head thrown back. Proudly conscious of the prime importance of his work he begins the age-old ritual that has not changed since Joseph's brethren were sent to buy corn in Egypt.

Dipping his right hand into the apron he takes up handful after handful and strides along scattering the grain in a wide semi-circle before him. Up and down the field he goes, hour after hour his heavy boots raising a trail of dust behind him. I trot along beside him as the seed falls evenly to right and left, and he tells me stories of the days when he was young.

Over there, beyond Loch Lene, is the high green hill of Knock Eyon, where his uncle was hanged as a rebel in 1798. He tells me of the horror of the Famine years, of how he had seen men too weak to stand, creeping on their hands and knees along the roadside, their mouths green with the juices of the grass they had been eating. And of the year his horses died and the plough lay idle, and he got five spades made in the forge, for himself and his sons and daughters, and of how they had set to work and dug up the field he was now sowing.

"We finished it in a month", he told me, "from headland to headland, but it nearly killed us".

Food On the Hillside

But now my father is yoking old Bob to the harrow, to break the clods and cover up the seed. The iron teeth of the harrow level down the crests of the ridges left by the plough, blanketing the seeds snugly under the fine earth. At mid-day the "sailor's jacket" appears through a rift in the clouds, and presently the spring sun shines out gloriously in the blue.

The air is filled with the song of the lark, and the scent of the rich flowering furze is all around us on the soft hillside breeze. My grandfather has finished the sowing and my mother has arrived with a basket of fresh wheaten bread, golden butter, and a steaming pitcher of hot tea. There is home-cured bacon, too, delicious to the taste, that cuts like butter.

My father has fed a bucket of oats to old Bob at the headland, and he himself now comes along wiping the sweat from his forehead. And we all sit down on the soft grass border to enjoy a meal with that hearty appetite which is the reward of hard work in the open air.

The Mountains are Clear

While my father is finishing the harrowing my grandfather is fencing a gap in the furze hedge to keep the neighbour's sheep from invading his domain. The sun is low in the west when he announces to me that it is "quitting time", and bids my father unyoke the horse. The old man's eyes wander to the eastern horizon. "The mountains are very clear this evening", he says to my father. "Rain to-night will do that field a power of good".

I turn in the direction of his gaze and there they rise in all their grandeur, dreamy blue and eighty miles away, the long line of the Wicklow mountains against the evening sky. And sure enough that night the rain came and it lasted all the next day and into the following night, but my grandfather was happy that the seed was in the earth.

Circuit of the Field

In three weeks' time after the gentle Spring rain, the brown hillside field was a carpet of emerald, and with the passage of the months the time of harvest came round. And one evening in August my grandfather said to my father:

"I will go up to the Bush Hill and see if the oats is fit to cut". He took me with him and we made a circuit of the field. Not alone did we go around the oats field, but we went around the bog gardens, past the pools that were sweet with water-lilies, and before our journey was done my grandfather and I had travelled together round the whole boundary of our little farm.

I did not know it then, but it was his last journey. He died the next day, as peacefully as he had lived.

And now I am back in the present again, having re-lived in memory that little scene of fifty years ago. All the actors are gone, their parts are played. Now they sleep together in the ancient churchyard of St. Feighin, under the rock of Fore, "quiet as a plough laid by at the furrow's end".

Mountain Sanctuary

That hill is holy since the day
When Moses trod its rugged road,
And heard, mid thunders, on Sinai,
The Ten Commands of God.

And holy is that other hill,
Where Simon Peter, James and John
Bowed down, as on their raptured eyes
Mount Thabor's blinding glories shone.

And Cruachan, too, is holy ground,
Where Patrick wept till stars grew pale
And from an Angel promise wrung
That Ireland's Faith shall never fail.

And in his care, till Judgement Day
Are all the children of the Gael.

The Man with Green Fingers

Of all the various jobs that fell to my lot on my father's hillside farm, the hardest of all was picking stones.

It was most back-breaking work and it was always done in the spring, just when the new meadow-grass was beginning to grow.

My job was to clear the ground of all the stones, usually about the size of potatoes, and carry them away in an old iron bucket to the nearest headland, and dump them there in a heap. This was to protect the keen blade of scythe from contact with them at hay-cutting time, or, if a mowing machine was being used, to prevent blades from being broken.

Now I never ceased to wonder where all the stones came from. Even though I raked the field from end to end, I never could succeed in clearing it to my father's satisfaction, for he always found a multitude after me the next day.

Silver Grace

I tried to explain to him that they must have grown up during the night, but he would have none of it. Eventually he would send me off to do something more congenial, and would finish the stone-picking himself, all the time loudly complaining to nobody in particular about the useless children he was blessed with - always stuck with their heads in books instead of helping him on the land.

However, his anger was short-lived, for when I came back to him again later in the evening, the stones were all picked, and he was studying with appreciative admiration the growth of a graceful silver deal which he had planted in a sheltered corner the previous autumn. He had found the medicine for heartache that lurks in lovely things, and was again at peace with the world.

Young Saplings

As far back as I can remember, my father was always planting young trees. His own father, who was hard set to provide for a numerous family during the terrible aftermath of the Famine years, had no time to shelter or beautify his treeless acres, so when my father came of an age to help, and times were easier, he set about planting with a will. He has what is known as green fingers, for every young tree and thornquick that he planted grew and flourished rapidly under his skilful hand.

I realise now that he missed his vocation, for he had all the natural ability and taste of a well-paid landscape gardener, but this was cramped by the fact that he had to toil all his life as a poor struggling farmer trying to make ends meet and never getting anywhere.

Many a time in childhood I heard him say to my mother, "A copper-beech would look well out there opposite the door" or "A horse-chestnut would set off that bare spot in the hedge," or "A lilac-bush would be lovely at the garden gate," and my mother would nod her head in agreement, and off he would go, maybe the next day, to some distant nursery that he would vaguely refer to as "up the County Meath" and come back with a selection of young saplings.

It was a rare pleasure to watch him planting these. He would handle them tenderly, like living things (which, of course, they were), spreading out their branching roots and fibres evenly with his fingers in the fine clay, and stamping the earth firmly round the stems with his heavy boots. Most important of all, he would ensure that the tender green shoots of the young trees were protected from marauding goats and inquisitive cows by a formidable palisade of thorny branches of hawthorn, driven into the ground all around the fragile sapling.

Prose And Poetry

It was my father's favourite recreation every Sunday after Mass to wander from field to field inspecting his young trees, and there

140

were dozens of them all around the ditches. We children, would straggle after him. Of course, he would cast an occasional glance at the crops, too, but I think the young trees were nearest to his heart. The crops represented the daily bread and butter, the prose, as it were, of life, but the lovely young trees were the poetry, the decoration of life, for he knew the truth of the maxim that "man does not live by bread alone".

Planting young trees gave him an opportunity for self-expression, for doing something creative, and he rejoiced in their growth, for he was a poet at heart. Besides, the life of the crops ended with the seasons, but a tree once planted could go on, maybe for centuries. But even among the trees he had his favourites, and during his Sunday afternoon ramble he would always pause where he had a young poplar planted in the farthest corner of an upland field nearest to the sky. After contemplating this poplar for a while he would turn around to enjoy the view.

From this green height, half of Ireland lay stretched out before him like a map. Here and there the shining white spire of a remote country church lifted itself into the blue air. "What a lovely place to be buried," he would say to me.

A Requiem

Eighty-odd years earlier he had been born into a bare hill-side farm without a tree or bush to shelter or beautify the little fields. He left it in High Summer, when the old home of his childhood was hemmed in on every side by a green arbour of trees in all their leafy pride. He had signed his name indelibly everywhere around him.

The thick hawthorn hedges that now bordered his fields were white and scented with the May-blossom and musical with the song of birds.

The quarter-mile stretch of boreen from his home to the red gate was now a shady avenue overhung by arching branches of ash and beech and chestnut, of plum and cherry and sycamore. Years before, he had unwittingly provided his own guard of honour for

141

this day, for now all these trees hung out their green banners like an arch of triumph over him as he passed underneath them for the last time, on his way to his final resting place in the ancient valley of Fore.

There is no headstone to mark the spot where he lies, but every year when the green miracle of Spring sweeps over the land, the horse-chestnuts that he planted long ago with loving hands lift aloft their thousand white candles for him, and the purple lilacs at the garden gate bloom for him again. And the soft hillside breezes that continually murmur through his delicate shining poplars, his glorious copper beeches and his treasured silver deals chant a perpetual requiem to the memory of the man with the green fingers who planted them there and loved them.

Glenasmole

Deep in the mountains' sheltered fold,
In scented calm of gardens old,
November burns red and gold!

An Eden here, where never blows
A wind to chill the budding rose
A vale that Winter never knows.

From morn to evening's crimson bars
Deep peace is here, and nothing mars
The night-long silence of the stars.

And beautiful beyond the moor,
The purple heights of wild Kippure,
With moonlight's magical allure!

Deep in the mountains' sheltered fold
In scented calm of gardens old
November burns red and gold!

A Holiday with Memories

There was a time when I used to look forward eagerly to seeing a new place each year.

I reasoned with myself: "Life is short, so why not see as much of this good green earth as possible during the little space of three score years and ten".

And so it was that I have seen many of the show places of the earth that I had read about and dreamed of since I was a child. But not all. There are many more places that I wanted to see and have not seen, places that must ever remain as poetry in my mind. But I am content, for as time goes on, I realise more and more that these faraway places hold no memories for me, and will not move me like the country of my childhood which now shines for me with the light that never was on sea or land. For I had the great good fortune to be born in a green and pleasant midland valley where nothing much has changed in the past fifty years, and where the longest life slips by like a fieldmouse, not shaking the grass.

An Island in the Bog

In a world of turmoil and change it is refreshing to escape to this green oasis in the heart of the hills, to see and hear again the sights and sounds of childhood, and to linger at the stiles that knew my morning dreams. One by one I recall from the ragbag of memory all those lovely things which made so delightful the summers of long ago. White water-lilies floating in their gay beauty on the black bog-pools. The almost inaccessible island in the bog where the rare green lizard used to sun himself in security. There also, were the blue eggs in the wild duck's nest, half hidden under a thicket of branchy bog heather, where my mother used to send me to pull a few strands to make a heather besom to sweep the kitchen floor.

To reach the island it was necessary to take off shoes and stockings and wade knee-deep through the bog. What a soothing sensation it was to feel the warm bog mud oozing up between one's toes. Talk of modern mud packs for beauty, a month in the bog barefooted was a certain cure for all foot ills. And then the soft swishing music of the wind through the clusters of swaying reeds, with here and there a great brown sceptre reed, stiff as a spear, standing up among them.

A Journey to the Well

A mile to two away was the well of Tobar-na-Gin where my mother would send me for a can of cold spring water to cool the butter after a churning in the heat of a long vanished summer day. Here for me was the very Fountain of Youth sought in vain by Ponce de Leon of old. The clear delicious water, bubbling up through the fine white sand, kept the smooth blue pebbles at the bottom of the well continually moving, and overflowed in a little stream, half hidden under a living carpet of bronze and green water-cress, into the nearby lake.

I still remember the dark green leaves of cabbage, plucked fresh from the kitchen garden and big as dinner plates, glistening with drops of water when rinsed, to hold the pats of yellow butter taken from the churn, and keep them cool in the barn which served my mother for a dairy. Floating in through the kitchen window came the sweet heady fragrance of the nigh-scented stocks after sunset, and the ragged petals of the big pink roses on the whitewashed wall outside, were a delight to the eye, their perfume surpassing all the scents of Araby.

Stolen Gallops

I used to envy my father, who always went to visit his friends on horseback. It was my job to saddle and bridle old Bob for him, and then lead the animal to the door, where my father would vault lightly from the rather high doorstep into the saddle. Fearing an accident, he would never allow me to mount the horse, and I could not convince him that I would not break my neck if I went out riding. But the urge was irresistible and I am afraid I often slipped out unknown to him.

I used to get up and dress at four o'clock on many a fine summer morning when everyone was asleep, steal out to the stable, and saddle and bridle old Bob, who always looked at me so reproachfully that I found it hard to meet his eye. I used to feel like apologising to him whenever I hauled him out of his comfortable stall at that unearthly hour. But maybe it was my own guilty conscience and perhaps old Bob did not really blame me as much as I imagined.

However, my scruples vanished very quickly when my feet were in the stirrups, and I was away up the hillside for an early morning gallop, my horse's hoofs leaving a dark green path across the grass, still covered with the silver dew of morning. Arrived at the hill-top I would draw rein and survey the scene just lit by the rising sun. Never did the landscape look lovelier than on these early morning rides. It was as if I were seeing it for the first time, there was a bloom upon everything, all the hills and woods and lakes stood out as it newly created and fresh from the Hand of God.

Landlords and Abbeys

Just below me lay island-studded Lough Lene - gem of the Midland lakes - incredibly blue in its setting of green hills, and beyond it on another hill-top loomed the great green fort of Ran-Dhun, from which Turgesius the Dane ruled and ravaged the countryside before he was drowned in Lough Owel.

All around me were the great memorials of the past, the cairn-crowned hills of Loughcrew where Ollamh Fodhla, the chief law-giver of ancient Ireland was buried, and nearby, a modern martyr, Blessed Oliver Plunket was born. A distant wooded hill on the horizon, over which a road ran, recalled a line of an old ballad which kept running through my head as I gazed: "They tumbled him out of his phaeton on the Hill of Knock-she-Ban". A bad landlord was ambushed there in the dark days of the Land War.

And down in the valley at my feet lay the magnificent walls and turreted battlements of the great Benedictine Abbey of Fore, though now roofless and open to the skies, its exquisitely carved cloister arches still beautiful as a wreck of Paradise.

I used to be afraid that my father would get up early some morning and discover the empty stable, but my luck held and he never found me out. Everyone was asleep, not a wisp of blue smoke from any chimney far or near, and I had those green and golden mornings all to myself.

As life goes on the memories of one's childhood grow stronger and brighter, and in the end all that is left to one is a sheaf of memories, fragile enough, it is true, but yet strong enough to last as long as life lasts. And because of all these fond memories, the country of my childhood will hold me to the end. Memories of a loving mother, memories of wandering babyhood, of shy and timid schooldays, of the first altar at which one prayed.

And that is why at holiday-time my heart turns, not to faraway places, but to the little twisting field-paths, running under ragged hedges and over crooked stiles, the way that I went to Mass and school when I was a child. There is the landscape that mixed with my heart when I was a boy.

A Joyous Wish

A sky of springtime blue above,
In summer or in winter weather,
A friendly heart, or one you love,
To tramp the hills together.

These are the joys I wish for you,
And may your heart forever thrill
To all the glories of the view
Gained from the top of every hill.

A Present for the Postman

The time of year when Autumn merged into Winter was a time of enchantment in the valley.

Thick hedges of dark green furze bordered the narrow hilly boreen on the way to school. On a foggy morning those hedges would be almost hidden beneath a great multitude of spiders' webs woven during the night, and which now hung like white fairy handkerchiefs from thorn to thorn.

Later on, when the sun broke through the mist, the dewdrops in the webs began to glisten like diamonds, and presently the twisting boreen became an avenue of sparkling lights. But only for a little while. As the sun grew stronger and the glorious pageantry began to fade, and by the time the grey-walled schoolhouse came into view, the sober green hedges had lost all their borrowed glory.

And I remember nights of white moon-lit fog when the whole landscape became strange and new. High above, on the slopes of the Ben, I used to watch the fog settle in the valley, blotting out the river and the little bog-gardens, burying all beneath a vast expanse of white wool, which took on the appearance of a great lake of water under the moon.

A Purple Atrocity

At the approach of Christmas my grandfather would begin to think about the few friends to whom he used to give presents, and the most important of them all was the postman. He never forgot the postman, though I doubt very much, remembering it now, if the postman was really satisfied with grandfather's taste in neckties.

He used to take me with him to the Christmas market in the nearby town and into the chief draper's shop there to choose a necktie for the postman. Grandfather spent a considerable time going through the numerous fancy boxes of ties that the assistant produced, one after another. Unable to come to a decision, in the end he would ask the advice of the "shop boy" as the drapers' assistants were

147

called in my young days. "Now, he's about your own age and size, and what do you think would be a nice tie for him? Pick me out something you'd like yourself, and I am sure it will suit him".

The shop boy would wrinkle his brows for a moment or two, looking exceedingly wise, as if pondering over some weighty decision, and then suddenly dive beneath the counter and produce some purple atrocity which he would recommend as just the very thing to make the postman happy. And my grandfather, good simple man, would allow himself to be persuaded by the shop boy who probably was in a hurry, anyway, as it was near Christmas, and there were far more important affairs to attend to than selecting a suitable tie for the postman.

A Free Catalogue

What a figure of romance the postman was as he came through the red gate every morning, in his uniform with red piping, and peaked cap like a French soldier. His roomy brown canvas bag slung over his shoulder, was usually bulging with letters and parcels for the dwellers in the valley. Many a morning I used to watch out for him with a hopeful heart when I would be expecting some monster catalogue that used to be given away free by the big English manufacturers of guns or watches or bicycles. There was no paper shortage then. I am writing now of the spacious days before the first World War.

I remember one morning I was expecting a particularly big catalogue of sports goods that I had applied for, and I was early afoot to watch for the postman. Finally he appeared at the red gate which spanned the boreen about a quarter of a mile from the house. He saw me in the distance and began waving the catalogue over his head, signalling me to come and get it. Evidently he had no letters that day for any of the houses farther long the way, and anyhow he was probably tired carrying my endless catalogues. In my eagerness and excitement for something new, I began to run as fast as I could, and covered the quarter of a mile from the house to the red gate in record time. I can still see the indulgent smile of the postman as he surrendered the coveted catalogue into my eager hands.

I used to pore for hours over all these catalogues, lying in the sun under the old apple-tree in our wild and weed-grown garden. Turning over page after glossy page with their hundreds of pictures of everything one could think of was a source of endless amusement to me. Three things I wanted ardently then, were a bicycle, a gun, and a watch, but I might as well have asked my father for the moon as for any of these things. He probably could not afford the price anyhow - one does not grow rich on a hillside farm - but this was small consolation to me, and my heart grew sick with hopes deferred. In later years I did acquire all those things, but then the thrill was gone.

An Imposing Woman

However, there were compensations, and one of these was a periodical visit to grandmama. Shortly before Christmas my mother would say: "I want you to go up with this letter to grandmama, and you may stay for a few days". Those visits were the high spots of my childhood, though my regard for grandmama was always tempered with a little fear. She was an imposing woman, and always reminded me somewhat of Queen Victoria as she looked in her later days. But she had a heart of gold.

The path by the bank of the river was the magic highway that led to her home about five miles away. I used to go across the fields and over the stiles, following the winding of the river through the water meadows. Here flourished the shining yellow buttercups with their rich glossy dark green leaves, their roots nourished forever by the sweet running water. Here in their season bloomed the water iris with their silky golden plumes waving on long green stems.

Now, in grandmama's farm there was a small field, known as the "fort field", for there was a rath in one corner. I used to accompany her down there where a huge grey stone was embedded in the ring of the fort, and she would gravely inform me that the fairies lived beneath the stone, pointing out at the same time a small fissure in the moss-covered limestone where, she alleged, they used to go in and out.

But there were other charms about a visit to grandmama. It was there I was allowed to read all the thrilling books that I did not have at home. She had an extensive collection also of bound volumes of old "Shamrocks" and "Irish Emeralds" which were full of exciting stories. It was there I first revelled in the Red Indian novels of Fenimore Cooper (I wonder who reads him now) and lived with the castaways on the desert island in "Swiss Family Robinson" and thrilled to the cloak and sword characters in the novels of Sir Walter Scott. And then there were the apples. Layers of apples would be left to ripen and sweeten in the haystack in the haggard, and many a fine red apple I devoured by stealth, savouring its sweetness with all the half guilty delight of eating forbidden fruit. Truly, there were apples of Eden.

But Christmas morning in the valley was a joy that never grew old. Going to early Mass in the dark frosty morning, and seeing the Christmas candles shining in the windows of the many invisible houses dotted across the hillside - and the stars shining in the night-blue sky above with equal brilliance - it was difficult to tell the candles from the stars. And there were many real hard frosts in the early winters of this century. I remember one such at Christmas when all the Midland lakes were frozen over, and one could drive a horse and cart across the ice. The heavy frost had fallen on Lough Lene in the night, freezing the music of its little lapping waves into silence, and it was a strange experience to see the lake one had always known as blue and laughing in the sunshine, now icebound and dead.

The frost lasted for a long time. Snow fell intermittently during the day, and by night the lake lay silent under the dull glow of the copper-coloured moon. But one night the wind changed to the south and the great thaw began. And with the thaw, came the sound of mighty waters being set free once more from their icy prison, and like a continuous roll of distant thunder for many days was the breaking and the melting of the massive sheet of ice that covered the waters of Lough Lene.

A Deserted Village

One of the joys of country life in the long dark winters of my childhood was the nightly ramble to the ceilidhe-house.

Certain houses in the parish were known as ceilidhe-houses, where the people were more sociable than in other houses, and where one neighbour after another would drop into the family circle in the evenings for a chat on local doings, the crops, the weather, the prices of cattle, the births, marriages, and deaths.

In this way, one remark would lead to another, one incident recall another, until the night passed, as if on wings.

Ritual of the pipe

To watch the old men filling their pipes around the cheerful turf fire in a ceilidhe-house was always a source of endless fascination to me. I remember one jovial old fellow who made a veritable ritual of the procedure night after night.

After selecting a comfortable seat in the warm chimney-corner, he would fumble in his pockets and eventually produce a blackened clay pipe and an old battered tin tobacco box containing the precious chunk of plug tobacco, and, with an equally disreputable-looking pen-knife, proceed to shave very thin slices off the plug into the palm of his left hand. Then, with empty pipe between his teeth, he would begin slowly rubbing the cut slices between his hands - the heel of the right fist rotating like a mill-stone in the cupped left palm-grinding the tobacco to the necessary fineness, all the time staring in to the fire with a far-away look, and the anticipation of joy to come lighting up his ancient eyes.

After that came the slow, restful, deliberate filling of the pipe with the prepared tobacco, lighting it by burying it bowl downwards in a red burning sod of turf, and then pulling vigorously until the tobacco was well alight, and tamped down with the shining tin lid. At last with closed eyes and a long sigh of relief he would settle

151

back comfortably to enjoy the rich luxury of his soul-satisfying nightly smoke.

He was an old bachelor, and once told me in a moment of confidence that his idea of the greatest happiness on this earth was "a full and well-drawin' pipe and no child cryin'."

The Cowslip Fields

The ceilidhe-house I loved best in the old days was one of a cluster of thatched houses, huddled together at the end of a short boreen, which opened out into the quiet of the cowslip fields and was known locally as Slieve-Dhu.

There were many more thatched houses in the Midlands fifty years ago than there are to-day, and now, of course, they do not build such houses any more.
The thick uneven walls were usually built of yellow clay made into mortar and mixed with chopped straw to bind it together. When the clay was set, the walls were whitewashed with lime inside and outside, and when newly thatched those houses looked very attractive, blending harmoniously with the green fields and brown bogs of Westmeath.

The materials of which they were built were all obtainable on the spot. The yellow clay was found a few feet down in the earth, the lime was made from the natural blue limestone, burned to a dazzling whiteness in the local limekiln, and, of course, the yellow straw for thatching was grown in the fields.

Moreover, those houses had the merit of being cool in summer and cosy and warm in winter, and had not the cold grey angular look of the many concrete houses we see to-day.

A Happy Family

The family in this favourite ceilidhe-house of my youth were four in number, two brothers, Jim and Dan - the hardest workers and neatest tillers of their fields in the whole parish - and two sisters, Anne and Maggie, all middle-aged and unmarried. Anne, the eldest, was the housekeeper, and literally a "spinster" for she was an expert also at her spinning wheel.

I never tired of watching her carding the rough grey natural wool from the sheep's back into a soft and silky heap, before spinning it into yarn for knitting the thick warm wool socks for her two hardworking brothers. Maggie was a dressmaker, and was usually kept busy "making" for the local belles.

Here the general conversation often ended up in a game of cards, but this game I could never master. But I learned to play draughts and enjoyed it, for Maggie was my teacher during the intervals she could snatch from her sewing machine. Jim, the eldest brother, rarely had any time to spare for card-playing, and in the pauses between the games when the cards were being dealt out, the regular sound of his flail could be heard from the adjoining barn, where he worked alone by the light of a candle threshing his oats by hand night after night.

They were the happiest family imaginable, and always lived in the greatest harmony, and the house was full of brightness and warmth during the long winter nights. The dancing light of the cheerful turf fire flickered back from the shining plates on the dresser, and the white-globed lamp hanging from the ceiling threw a warm glow over the laughing, good-humoured company.

The Silence of Death

It was so pleasant after saying good-night to ramble home across the fields by the still and ghostly hedges, to my grandmother's house, listening to the sound of soft breathing where the cattle were asleep in the darkness around me.
 Waiting for me by the hearth-stone would be a warm supper of freshly-cooked oatmeal stirabout, tasty and sweet as a nut when mixed with new milk. Oh! the flavour of oatmeal stirabout and fresh milk, especially when the meal came newly-ground from the mill after the harvest.

During the the long years I have been away from my native home I often wished to revisit Slieve Dhu and see again the ceilidhe-house of my youth, and to see how time had dealt with the kindly heart I knew there, but the opportunity did not come my way until one evening last harvest, when I turned down the old familiar boreen, which seemed to have grown more narrow and crooked that I had remembered it.

A strange silence was in the air as I picked my steps along the muddy cart-track. I did not know it then, but it was the silence of death. A tumble-down heap of ruins was all that met my eye at the end of the lane. A friendly face peering through a hedge inquired if I was looking for anybody. I stared at him blankly, for I did not know him, but he told me he remembered me, though he was only a child at the time. And then he told me he was the only inhabitant left of this once populous village in the fields, a nephew of one of the old people I knew.

Honest, Homely Faces

It was only then I realised that I had been too long away, and I fell to thinking of all that had happened during the long years of my absence. And in my mind I could see it all. I pictured each friendly face I knew, at the end of a laborious and God-fearing life, being waked in the best room under a canopy of white sheets starred with crosses of shining green laurel leaves, and with all the holy pictures in the house ranged around the bed.

I could see their honest homely faces, weather-beaten from a lifetime of labour in the fields, take on something of the majesty of marble when laid out one by one in the brief dignity of death. There would be rosaries said for their souls in the calm light of blessed candles, there would be clay pipes and tobacco and snuff and holy water, according to the custom of the wakes I remembered in my youth. And over there across the fields in the rich tangled grass and holy earth of the ancient churchyard of Killalon, they would be laid to rest at last.

I do not know how long I lingered remembering them all. But twilight was falling as I turned away, and the same old harvest moon of my childhood was now shining calmly down on the roofless walls of yellow clay, and the crumbling gables of the little village that died in the quiet of the cowslip fields.

A Memory

"I remember your mother going to school
I remember her well", said he,
"She was dressed in green and had yellow hair
And a comely face to see",
And my heart went out to the kind old man
Whose words brought joy to me.

"I mind how her answers pleased the priest,
When she won a prayer book prize,
I mind the day that I spilled the ink
All over her exercise,
And she reddened up to the roots of her hair,
And the tears stood in her eyes".

And he filled his pipe and recalled those scenes
Of interest only to me,
Eager for news of the mother I loved,
And wishing that I could see
With eyes of mine what he had seen,
And knowing it could not be.

And yet, and yet, as he pulled on his pipe,
While he pictured that school-room bare,
I could see through his eyes a rustic child
In the desk at her lessons there,
With ink-stained fingers, and wild-rose cheeks
And a wisp of yellow hair.

The Death of Pope Leo XIII

It was a quiet Summer evening well-nigh fifty years ago. My mother was coming up from the pasture where she had been milking, carrying a big tin can of foamy milk in her left hand, her right arm outstretched to help to balance the heavy can on the other side.

As I watched her coming across the field path I could see a look of sadness in her face. She was usually smiling, but as she drew nearer I could see there were tears in her eyes.

"I've just heard from Old Rosie that the poor Pope is dead", she said softly. Old Rosie lived a few hundred yards away, and was what is known in the country as a good neighbour, always ready with a kind word and a smile and a helping hand in time of trouble.

News travelled slowly in those days to that quiet Midland valley hidden away in a fold of the hills. Old Rosie must have heard it from someone who had been to Castlepollard, the nearest town. Later, my father also came in with the news. He had heard it over in Ankerland, a little roadside village a mile or so away across the fields. He, too, looked concerned, and then my mother said, "Now, children, it's time to stop playing and come in, and we'll say the Rosary for the Pope", and we all knelt down very devoutly that lovely summer evening, and said our childish prayers for the eternal repose of the soul of Leo XIII.

Bordered In Black

Later on in the week a newspaper trickled in from somewhere, and it was all bordered in black, and there was hardly any other news in it except about the Pope - how he was born as far back as 1810, the son of an Italian nobleman, Count Pecci, elected to the Throne of Peter in his late sixties, and after a long and fruitful reign of twenty-five years he was now dead at the age of ninety-four.

On the following Sunday he was prayed for at Mass in the Chapel of Fore, and the parish priest preached a sermon about him, stressing the great loss he was to the Church and requesting the congregation to pray that God would send a worthy successor before long to the widowed Church. And God did.

Eldest Of Eight

But this time it was a very different man, and all through the following weeks the papers carried the very exciting story of the election of a new Pope, Cardinal Sarto by name, who was the son of a very poor man, indeed.

The new Pope was the eldest of the eight children of the post-master of a poor Italian village call Riese who, badly paid, found it very difficulty to support his large family. Yet he was destined to be the father of the great Pius X, whose eventual canonisation is now spoken of.

But this particular Papal elections was very remarkable for the fact that there was an attempt to use the Veto in the Conclave on behalf of the Emperor of Austria, who feared the election of Cardinal Rampolla, Secretary of State to Leo XIII. Now, the Veto was the alleged right of the rulers of certain Catholic countries to object to the election of a Cardinal of whom they did not approve. This right was never really recognised by the Church, and the assembled Cardinals asserted their independence by increasing their votes for Cardinal Rampolla.

However, in the end, after many ballots, Cardinal Sarto was elected Pope, and one of his first acts, when he came to the Throne was to abolish the alleged right of Veto forever.

All this news made the headlines when I was young, in the early years of this century. They were long years of peace, that only came to an end amid the thunder of the guns of the first world war in 1914.

These early memories came back to me with a rush lately, when wandering around inside the mighty Basilica of Saint John Lateran in Rome, I paused to read an inscription on the door of a Papal tomb. The words I read were "Leo XIII Pont. Max." and looking upwards, there, sure enough, stood the great Pope himself, a majestic marble figure in full flowing vestments with the triple crown on his head, whose death had brought the tears to my mother's eyes nearly fifty years before.

And at the sight, a casement opened on eternity, the past became the present, as deeply moved I stood there realising that time meant nothing after all, and glimpsing the profound truth of the scriptural saying that a "thousand years in the sight of God is but as one day".

The same feeling came over me again in Saint Peter's - that tremendous temple with its acres of floor space that dwarf all human beings to the size of pigmies - when I saw the rugged, homely features of Pius X in sculptured marble of heroic size looking down from his niche in the painted walls.

He lived through that period of peace I have already spoken of, and died of a broken heart, it was said, because he laboured so hard for peace, but was unable to prevent the first world war.

Past and Present

But, above all, when the living Pope himself, "the Holy Lord of Rome", was borne up the aisle of Saint Peter's on the shoulders of his twelve red-robed attendants, the sense of timelessness, of past and present blending, was supreme. Seeing him, all the long line of dead Popes back through the centuries, all the Leos and Clements and Gregories, whose colossal statues adorn the walls around, seem to come to life again and be embodied in that slender figure in white, the latest of them all and destined to go down in history among the greatest.

And I fell to thinking of the many crowned heads of Europe who have been toppled from their thrones since I was a boy. The thrones of Portugal and Spain, of Germany and Italy are all gone. The Austrian Empire and its ruler, powerful enough in my youth to attempt to sway a Papal election, are gone too.

But the oldest dynasty in the world, the Papal dynasty of peace, still remains, tracing back its unbroken lineage through all the centuries of blood and war to that far-off day twenty hundred years ago when the bearded fisherman first heard the Divine commission ringing in his ears "Thou art Peter". And it will remain to the end to keep reminding us that spiritual things are eternal, and temporal things transient, that we are only pilgrims here, and "all our life is but a wandering to find a home, and when we're gone, we're there".

And so it was that Rome woke again in me the half-forgotten memories of youth, and sent my thoughts roving back to a Summer twilight nearly fifty years ago, and a gentle mother with tears in her eyes because the Pope was dead.

Waiting for the Last Bell

Every Sunday morning there is a pleasant interlude - not unknown, of course, in other Irish country parishes - outside the chapel gate of my native parish of Fore.

About half an hour or so before Mass is due to begin, groups of young men and boys, and older men, too, gather on the green grassy roadside slope outside, in the shadow of the ancient town gate. It is a definite social occasion, when neighbours who may not have met since the previous Sunday come together once again, and discuss the state of the crops, the prospects of fine weather, all the small change of conversation peculiar to men of the fields, whose talk tends to run in much the same channel from generation to generation.

This period of recreation is known as waiting for the last bell.

Of course, the women and girls, as befits the more devout sex, do not linger at all. They pass demurely through the crowd into the church, where a few pious old men and women, who feel their day is drawing to a close, and whose thoughts are on a better world than this, are already dotted among the seats, fingering their beads.

But the big majority linger outside waiting for the last bell, leaning over the low stone walls, laughing quietly at each other's jokes, all the time idly gazing across the hills and fields they have known all their lives. For the grey-blue limestone church stands in a lovely green valley, which daily viewed, pleases daily, and whose novelty survives long knowledge and the scrutiny of years.

Moving among this congenial crowd one Sunday morning lately, I came upon a stranger from a neighbouring county who asked me if I could tell him something of the seven wonders of Fore.

Remembering as best I could what I had learned from my grandfather, I began: "You must remember that nearly all the wonders are connected with the great Saint Fechin, who founded a church and monastery in this pleasant valley over thirteen hundred years ago. Soon he had assembled round him a big community of three hundred monks who were attracted by his holy life.

"Now his holy well is over there in a little green field between the ruins of his church and monastery. It is overshadowed by a very ancient triple-branched ash tree and an elder bush studded with medals and beads, pins and crosses, and festooned with bits of coloured string, humble mementoes of countless pilgrims."

"According to an ancient tradition, the waters of this well will not boil, nor the wood of the ash tree burn. These are two of the wonders of Fore. Mind you, I have never tried to boil the water or burn the wood; if any heretic likes to do so, he may, but I would not like to be the person waiting for that particular water to boil over that particular ash tree fire."

"Further over beyond the well is the third wonder, the ruins of an abbey built on a 'shaking scraw,' that is, boggy land, where normally a firm foundation could not be obtained for the mighty walls to stand upon."

"The fourth wonder is the ruined mill without a stream, that is, without water to turn it. The monks found it so difficult to grind enough wheat for such a large community in their stone hand-querns, that their abbot, St. Fechin, caused a water-mill to be built. When this was done, the builder discovered that there was no water in the neighbourhood at a high enough level to turn the wheel. But the saint was not dismayed. At the head of his monks he went in procession chanting hymns across the high green hill - now called Windtown - which rises between the valley of Fore and the shore of Loch Lene. Coming to a rocky place at the edge of the lake, he raised his staff like another Moses, and still praying, struck the rock."

"At the stroke, the rock split, the waters of Loch Lene went rushing through the cleft and out underneath the hill, finally emerging the other side to turn the mill-wheel. This underground river is flowing strongly from that day to this, and is the fifth wonder of Fore. In fact, the drinking water of the village comes from this miraculous torrent."

"Up there, near the base of the towering rock, is the sixth wonder, the narrow cell of the last anchorite, or hermit, in Ireland. He died about 1616, but his hermitage has been converted into a mausoleum or tomb for the Earls of Westmeath."

"The seventh and last wonder is the mighty sculptured stone over the doorway of the ancient church of St. Fechin, just below the village. This stone was so heavy and unwieldly that the workmen, when building the church, were unable to lift it, so the saint sent them off for a meal. When they returned they found the stone lifted into its place, where it still remains to this day."

"When you go into Mass presently you will see a stained glass window behind the high altar depicting this miracle of Saint Fechin lifting the stone into its place, assisted by angels. And if you want to know any more details about the ancient ruins in this quiet valley just go down the village street, where you will see a name in Gaelic over a shop-door. There lives Mr. Gillooly, who knows far more about the antiquities of Fore that I do, aye, and even more that the learned societies from Dublin who come here occasionally."

But suddenly the Sabbath calm is shattered by the mighty crash and clamour of the last bell from the blue-grey limestone spire, the signal that the priest is already vested for the altar.

With a noisy shuffling of heavy boots on the gravel of the chapel yard the congregation begins to move in. My newfound friend and I move with them. The bell keeps on ringing, imperious, insistent, commanding, drowning our voices in great vibrating waves of sound that break on the ear like a summons from another world, forcibly raising all men's thoughts from things temporal to things eternal.

Holy Poverty

At morning Mass he's always there
Grey-haired and old, infirm and poor,
And humbly in a corner bare
He kneels, unnoticed and obscure.

And at the Consecration Hour
Bows low, for miracle is done,
When at the priestly words of power
Comes down from Heaven the Holy One.

Now at the rails, "My God adored",
He prays "Forgive me all my wrong",
While weeping, "I'm not worthy, Lord",
The White Host rests upon his tongue.

Transfigured now, no longer poor,
But inly rich beyond all measure,
He rises radiant, heavenly-sure,
Within his heart, the world's Treasure.

Hands clasped in prayer, past lights and flowers,
He moves with reverence to his place,
While the light of a lovelier Land than ours
Long lingers in his face.

Marriage in the Midlands

As a student of human nature, I have always been interested in what makes people marry each other, but I have never solved the problem to my own satisfaction, for it is still true, as Meredith says, that "women do not dare to be spontaneous" in this matter. They must wait till they are asked.

Long ago in the country I knew a faded old maid, whom nine out of ten men would pass by, and yet the tenth married her and found in her all his heart could desire. I knew another couple, neighbours' children, who had gone to school together, but evinced no particular interest in each other until both were well over forty, and then suddenly discovered they were in love. They, too, grabbed their happiness before it was too late and got married.

In my native countryside the marriage rate is rather low, and the men who marry, do not, as a rule go far afield for their wives. It is a country of small farmers, who are by no means poor, with here and there a few richer ones. Match-making was still common there in my young days and one of the chief qualifications of the bride-to-be was that she should have a good knowledge of the work necessary to be done around a farmer's house, and the energy and ability to do it, plus a reasonable "fortune" as the dowry was called. If she was good-looking, all the better, but it was not essential.

The fortune required varied with the size of the farm of the prospective bridegroom. And another thing, in match-making there was no nonsense about love. Didn't I often hear old Lizzie Kavanagh proclaim to all and sundry coming from Mass, in reference to a very wealthy and eligible farmer of many acres that "no woman would ever sleep under his roof unless she had a fortune of five hundred pounds." As old Lizzie herself was his housekeeper and did his washing, it is to be presumed that she had first-hand knowledge of her master's demands. I have since learned that he died some time ago, at an advanced age - still a bachelor.

Occasionally a man would do his own wooing, like another old farmer I remember. He too was wealthy, but somewhat eccentric. "I have a heart like Wolfe Tone" he used to say to a young country girl of my acquaintance when pressing her to marry him. I regret to say in spite of such a patriotic recommendation, he had to take his heart elsewhere. But he did in fact find a young wife eventually, who promptly married him, it was rumoured, for his money and his land. He did not live very long and his now rich young widow soon consoled herself with a man nearer to her own age.

And there was old Peter. How well I remember him coming across the bog to a widow's house I knew very well in my childhood. One evening as I opened the half door I could hear old Peter's rather gruff voice addressing the widow in the kitchen inside: "He doesn't want a dandy" and my curiosity was aroused instantly for I sensed that Old Peter was a go-between in looking for the hand and heart of the widow's pretty young daughter.

I took a seat in the chimney-corner, and the people of the house probably thought I was too young to take any notice of what was going forward, for I was allowed to remain while Old Peter continued to praise extravagantly this man whom the widow or her daughter had never ever seen.

The man who didn't want a dandy was a middle-aged man from the next parish, who had worked hard for a rich neighbouring farmer all his life and saved his money, and had just then bought a house and farm of his own. Some of Old Peter's phrases come back to me, "a very dacent, honest man", "a man of principle", "hardworking", "sober", " as quiet as a child", and the strange thing was that everything that was then said about this paragon of perfection turned out later to be perfectly true, for the widow's daughter married him after a short courtship, and actually lived happily ever after.

And now a curious thing occurs to me. In those days a proposal of marriage preceded the courtship. Nowadays, a proposal of marriage is, or should be, the sequel.

But marriage was not always so successful. Old Pateen and his sister Bess lived together in a one-roomed, mud-wall cabin a few fields away from my home. They had a small garden, which was kept neatly tilled, and the old brother and sister managed to scrape up a living by feeding a pig or two on the produce of the garden.

To give Old Pateen his due, he kept his house and garden very tidy, or "nice and purty," which was a favourite phrase of his, though he himself, I always felt, had something sinister about him. He had a profile like Judas in da Vinci's "Last Supper," hooked nose, short grey beard and malevolent eye. However, Bess and he lived together harmoniously enough. But one day in chance conversation somebody mentioned Old Pateen's wife. I was very young at the time, and I never knew till then that he had a wife.

When I enquired from my elders where she was, I was told that he was a "bad head to her," a euphemism used in my young days for a husband who ill-treated his wife. So she was now living apart from him with her relatives in the neighbouring town, and Old Pateen, to my childish wonderment, was apparently quite content to live and die with his sister Bess, without ever seeking a reconciliation with the woman he had married. I could not understand it at all.

But perhaps he was not altogether to blame that everything was not "nice and purty" in his past, for I often heard him quote and old Gaelic proverb which lists three things that drive the good man out of his house, "a leaky roof, a smoking chimney, and a scolding wife."

Then there was the mysterious glamour of the uniform for some women. In this case it was the old Royal Irish Constabulary, who were stationed in every little village in the Midlands and whose trim, well set up figures caused many feminine hearts to beat faster.

I remember in my youth a rather bookish young woman, a neighbouring farmer's daughter, who was enamoured of a particularly dashing specimen of the Force, and would refer to him as "my Hercules."

166

Somebody has said that "happiness in marriage is a piece of luck that sets your trembling," but from my observation of marriage in the Midlands, happiness is not looked for directly but if the other qualifications are there, similarity of religion, and background and upbringing, they form a suitable seed-bed for "the delicate flower of happiness to grow up with the years." And when "their hearts are of each other sure," happiness is the by-product of a successful marriage.

And I think of the many married couples I have known in my youth who had grown old together. I see them now, in the evening of their days, she pottering around her kitchen and her fowl, he out in the fields, mending a gap in the fence perhaps, seldom speaking much but yet a mutual support and comfort to each other, as if yoked together and ploughing the same furrow.

How often have I seen an old countryman coming in from the fields after his day's work, and finding his aged wife temporarily missing, maybe because she is only out milking the cows, look anxiously around him and become visibly uneasy until her re-appearance re-assures him that she is still poking around.

They have grown old together and become indispensable to one another, and very often when death comes to either, the one who is left does not linger too long, because, for the survivor "there is now shadow forever, where once there was sun."

Allen Wind

"The Bog of Allen wind is blowing
And it will bring the rain"
An old man warned my love and me
Tramping the mountain lane.

"The way is long to old Kilbride
And when the rain comes down
You'll have no shelter on that path
Through wastes of heather brown".

But no rain came on that glad day -
Strange light lay on the land,
As mile on mile to lone Kilbride
We wandered hand in hand.

Spring skies were blue above Slieve Bawn,
Black lambs leaped in the sun,
Bright eyes of love looked up to mine,
And our two souls were one.

Alone I tramp that lane to-day
Now Spring is here again,
The Bog of Allen wind is blowing
Upon my cheeks as then,
But now its knife is in my heart
and in my eyes, the rain.

Invitation

The heather is out on the Wicklow Hills
So come! My love, away!
Where the miles of Tyrian purple roll
From Seskin to Loch Bray.

Where the rowan berry hangs burning red
O'er the amber lake below
and the mosses cover the mighty stones
Of a thousand years ago.

We'll rest where the shy blue fraughan hides
'Neath the pines where the breezes sigh
And we'll dream of love in idleness
While the sun goes down the sky.

Nor ever remember the distant town
And its rumour of far-off wars
Till the harvest moon is above Slievebawn
And the lake is a shield of stars.

The miles of Tyrian purple roll
From Seskin to Loch Bray
For the heather is out on the Wicklow Hills
So come! my love, away!

Lough Lene

A quaint old market house, like a strayed spectator from another age, used stand midway in the old-world square of Collinstown. This charming and restful village on the bus road from Dublin to Granard is the gateway to Lough Lene, loveliest of the Westmeath Lakes.

Lough Lene under the summer sun is a blue and sparkling gem about three miles long and half that distance wide, set in a jig-saw pattern of incredibly green fields sloping away to wooded uplands.

The little fields are intersected by ragged hedges of creamy-white hawthorn, mingled with rich yellow furze, and the changing colours of hedge and field and sky are eternally reflected in the clear mirror of the lake.

Three islands

Three wooded islands adorn the lake, Monk's Island, Nun's Island and Castle Island. The latter is so called because a King of Meath, a benefactor of St. Columcille, once had his castle there.

One of the finest ecclesiastical bells ever found in Ireland was discovered about eighty years ago on Castle Island. Some fishermen were clearing away stones to make a landing place for their boat when the bell was found. It is made of cast bronze, quadrangular in shape, like the cowbells of Switzerland, only much larger and heavier. A lightly incised Celtic Cross decorates both faces of the bell, and a band of fret pattern in delicate lines runs round the base.

The Bell of Lough Lene is now in the National Museum, and the authorities there date it back to the 10th century (Incidentally, there is evidence to suggest that the distinctive design of the herd bells in use on the Continent today was originally copied from the bells carried by the ancient Irish missionaries who evangelized many parts of Europe before the Middle Ages).

One other fact may be of interest. The solid silver bell in use on the Ceann Comhairle's table in the Dail is a replica in half size of the Bell of Lough Lene. It was presented by Mrs. Cooper, in memory of her late husband, Major Brian Cooper.

A tyrant

The shores of Lough Lene are heavy with history. On one side of the lake rises the great fort of Randhun, where Turgesius, the "famous royal Dane" of the local ballad, ruled the natives during the Danish occupation in the 9th century. According to the ancient Gaelic chroniclers Turgesius was a most oppressive tyrant who extorted a tribute of an ounce of gold yearly from every householder under his dominion. If the gold was not forthcoming he punished the offender by cutting off his nose, so this tribute was known among the Irish as "airgead srona" that is "nose money".

On a recent visit to Randhun I tried to elicit some more information about Turgesius from a local shepherd whom I encountered on the high green slopes of his ancient fortress. All he could tell me was that the Danish tyrant came to a fitting end by being captured and imprisoned in a barrel and thrown in to the deepest of the neighbouring lakes.

On the opposite shore from Randhun is the miraculous cleft in the rock which appeared in answer to the prayers of the great St. Fechin causing the waters of Lough Lene to rush underground beneath the Rock of Fore and emerge in that historic valley to turn a mill built by the Saint where no water was available.

The underground torrent still rushes but to no advantage, for the mill is in ruins today.

The legends

And then there were the legends of the lake, told by the old people around the winter fires of home. According to them, Lough Lene too had its "round towers of other days" buried deeply in its clear waters. And the drownings also were remembered and retold. One in particular remained in my memory, about a poor man who lost his way at nights in the fields around the neighbouring lake, and was found drowned in the lakeside reeds the next morning with his jacket turned inside out, in a last despairing gesture to placate the unseen presences that had led him astray.

Lough Lene has been "discovered" since my young days, and the once quiet stretch of beach where I first learned to dive and swim is now transformed into a miniature Lido during the summer months. Bathers and swimmers come from all parts and the sun-warmed "fox sand" that forms the bed of the lake at this point is very easy on tired feet.

Lough Lene

'Twas here I was born and here I come
Who has roamed the wide world's ways
And I ask no better gift from God
Than here to end my days
To end my days where my life began -
My life of sun and rain -
In sight of my father's limestone hills
And the green shores of Lough Lene.

My father he toiled for many a year
Yet little of gold had he,
But he left me his love for the timeless things
Like the beauty of a tree -
White lilies agleam on the dark bog pools -
Wild roses after the rain -
And the wash of the waters white and blue
On the green shores of Lough Lene.

He left me his love for the summer eves
When the torch of the setting sun
Burns red and gold on the glassy calm
Of the lake when the day is done
And the blue fades slowly from the sky
As homeward wings the crane
While the sunset gilds the woods and hills
Round the green shores of Lough Lene.

Homeward to Memories

This is the season when many half-forgotten faces appear again at Sunday Mass in little country churches up and down through Ireland.

Sometimes it is the face of a bearded priest on the altar, pale with the tropic sun, more often the features of a couple of strangely - habited nuns in the congregation; but generally they are natives of the parish, come back for a brief holiday after an absence of ten, twenty, or maybe thirty years in a foreign land.

They arrive unobtrusively with the general body of tourists, travelling light with the minimum of luggage, having freed themselves long ago from that tyranny of the unessential which clutters up most of our lives.

Usually they remain for a couple of months, staying with relatives or friends, and depart again, like the swallows, as quietly as they came. Each of them is a soldier in that unconquerable army of Irish missionaries now scattered all over the world.

It was once my happy fortune to accompany two such nuns on a visit to their native parish after an absence of twenty-five years. I had known them as schoolgirls; they were "neighbours' children".

They had visited Rome and Lourdes on their journey home, and now they were back in the peace and tranquillity of their native Midlands in the beautiful lake country of north Westmeath.

Having been greeted by their relatives and friends with outstretched arms and happy tears, and been entertained with truly Irish hospitality, their first thought was of a visit to their "home from home" as they called it, the little church of their childhood.

They noticed and enjoyed every little sight and sound as they went along; sweet-peas in a cottage garden, like a rainbow tangled in a hedge, a straggle of inquisitive cows coming home to be milked, the fragrance of the lavender coloured stocks, jackdaws chattering in the presbytery trees.

It was fascinating to notice how much they delighted in the little things, even while their thoughts were habitually fixed upon the great ones - the true source of their happiness. Under the spell of their loving enthusiasm, things long familiar to me took on a fresh and new enchantment when seen through their eyes.

How happy they were to find that nothing had altered in that lovely old church on the shore of Lough Lene where they first knelt to pray, and where their parents and grandparents had knelt before them.

They had lingered long before the glorious stained-glass windows of Chartres, and marvelled at the priceless statuary of Rome, and yet they were far more thrilled to see again the flowing blues and reds of the little shining windows depicting the Agony and the Resurrection, above the high altar, in this ancient chapel of their dreams.

And they pointed out delightedly to each other, with happy cries of recognition, the plump twin cherubs, their wings tipped with gold, on either side of the chancel arch, still looking out with wide innocent eyes over the heads of the congregation.

Half surprised and wholly delighted to find that Time had stood still here, in a world of change, they were like pilgrims refreshed, gazing around in the temple of their vow. For it was in this small church while they were yet in their teens, kneeling before this well-remembered altar and rood, they first heard in their souls that mysterious and heart-shaking invitation "Leave all and follow Me"!

But what of all the missionaries, who for one reason or another, never get the chance to come home, although, they too, would give a lot "for a glimpse of the crags of Kerry or a whiff of the Galway air"?

The answer may be found in a scrap of a poem, written many years ago by a young nun in India, describing the life-long wish of here aged Reverend Mother to see the Ireland of her girlhood once again before she died.

It was not to be, however, and the poet depicts the saintly old nun at the end - her life drawing peacefully to its close in the midst of her labour of love - still dreaming vainly of home.

Mother Anthony, thinking, thinking,
"This year - next year - so much to do"-
And Ireland, sinking, sinking,
sinking into the westward blue!

Hymn to Blessed Oliver Plunket

O Blessed Martyr, hear our prayer,
Thine Irish children on thee call,
Make strong our Faith, again assailed;
Keep us true, whate'er befall,
And when the test comes, grant that we
May hold our Faith steadfast like thee.

By all the long and dreary days
And nights you lay in prison cell,
By all the hours you knelt in prayer
And vanquished all the powers of hell -
O Blessed Martyr, grant that we
May keep our Faith steadfast like thee.

By all the torment you endured
On that long road of agony,
When dragged through London's alien streets
From Tower Hill to Tyburn Tree -
O Blessed Martyr, grant that we
Be faithful unto death like thee.

The Midland Fair

It was always the same picture I used to see through my little bedroom window on awakening. Green fields stretching away for miles to a wooded horizon, where the stately towers of Clonyn Castle rose to view on the right, and on the left, the slender spire of Delvin pierced the morning sky.

During the long years of childhood this castle and spire rising from among the distant trees were the outposts of my little world, the ends of the earth. Everything beyond that skyline was a subject for imagination, and full of profound mystery. And that is why the charming midland village of Delvin holds a special place in my heart, for the spire of its lovely little Gothic church and the grey twin towers of Clonyn Castle are engraved on my memory forever. To revisit Delvin now in after years is the most restful thing I know: this quiet Westmeath village where it is always afternoon.

The seas of rich green grass roll up almost to the back doors of the houses, and in the summer time the scented sweetness of new-mown hay is heavy in the streets. Nobody ever seems to be in a hurry, there is always time for a laugh and a chat when one goes into the bright and well-stocked shops, and the business of buying and selling is conducted in a leisurely civilised fashion, very refreshing to the mind and body after the rush and scramble of shopping in the city.

At the upper end of the town stand the massive towers of another ancient castle built by Hugh de Lacy after the Norman invasion. Everything those old Norman barons built, whether castle, fortress, or cloistered abbey, was built for eternity, and the walls of Delvin Castle, over which hundreds of years have already passed, appear to be as everlasting as the Pyramids.

But there are a few days throughout the year when the village wakens up from its lotus-dream and there is a sound of tumult and shouting in the streets, and the air resounds to the lowing of close-packed herds of cattle, and the bleating of a multitude of sheep.

And if you are a stranger and would know how many days in each year the fair of Delvin is held, you must consult Old Moore's Almanac. Ah! What memories does that name evoke. Old Moore was a necessity in every farmer's house in Westmeath when I was young. My father used to buy it every Christmas for a few pence. It was sold by ballad-singers at the Christmas market of Castlepollard, and it was carefully preserved and consulted regularly all through the following year.

It had a pale green paper cover, and inside the front page was a quaint wood-cut of an incredibly old gentleman leaning heavily on a stick. He had a most mournful expression on his face, as if he was weighed down with all the sorrows of the world. Underneath the picture was printed the truly magnificent name "Theophilus Moore". No wonder he was mournful under the weight of such a name, for was he not the famous prophet who rarely saw the silver lining alleged to be in every cloud, and his predictions were mostly gloomy.

But Old Moore's Almanac was a most useful book for all that. It contained much weather lore, like the changes of the moon, and its weather forecasts were valuable enough in those pre-radio days. It had also much useful information bearing on the welfare of domestic animals. Besides it had plenty of room for a selection of verses from rural poets. But one of its chief merits was a complete list of all the fairs of Ireland. And there it was recorded that the fair of Delvin is held on the first Friday of each month.

It was my good fortune to arrive by chance the evening before the fair, and the native air went to my head like wine when I reached the village. Strong portable wooden barricades were being erected on the pavement outside each shop window. The place seemed to be preparing for a siege. And the next morning I knew the reason, for I was awakened by the trampling of innumerable cattle under my window.

Dressing hastily, I was soon in the thick of the crowds. All around me were the men from the fields with cattle to sell, and the buyers from here, there and everywhere with money to buy. "What did you come to the fair for"?, a buyer with a strong County Cavan

177

accent ironically inquired of a bashful country youth who had just refused his offer for a good-looking heifer. And as the would-be buyer walked away, another man appeared on the scene to inquire solicitously "What did he bid ye"? The youth told him, and the self-appointed bargain-maker or "tangler" as he is called, dashed away after the buyer and dragged him back again. He came back loudly protesting that the heifer was not worth one penny more. And then another "tangler" joined in, imploring both buyer and seller to "split the difference".

To a stranger it would be most amusing to see these "tanglers" trying to catch hold of the hand of both buyer and seller, and drag them together at all costs trying to clinch the bargain. Sometimes they would succeed, sometimes they would fail. The energy these cattle buyers display is prodigious, as they must reach the fair from many miles away early in the morning, if they want the pick of the animals. As I watched them I decided the job would be too strenuous for me, and the part of a looker-on was much easier to play, though of course, not so profitable. I consoled myself by saying "money isn't everything". When a sale is concluded, the buyer produces either a stick of red or blue raddle to mark the animals as his own, or else a little scissors to make a cut in some distinctive fashion through the hair.

"Well, if you don't buy them, you won't have them to sell", an old cattle-jobber remarked, as he gave his own special scissors-cut to half a dozen fine animals he had just bought.

All the day long the fair went on, and towards evening, a young fellow arrived with an accordion and the strains of "Galway Bay" mingled with the lowing of the cattle in the street. Later on, as the fair began to get thin, people appeared at their doors with buckets of water and sloshed them on the pavement. Shortly afterwards some of the wooden barriers before the shops were taken away, and by degrees the village began to resume its former appearance. Next day the long street would be swept clean once more. And so the rhythm of life goes on from fair to fair. The fair is a social occasion too, and farmers meet each other and talk together animatedly upon subjects that interest farmers. After a day spent at the fair I was glad enough to mount my bicycle in the evening and get out again on the quiet roads that wander in all directions from the village, pausing here and there at rustic stiles that knew my morning dreams.

It was late when I returned from visiting some friends farther down the country, and peace had fallen once more on the quiet street. The village itself was in darkness, only a faint red glow from the Sanctuary lamp shone through the windows of the silent church. The sound of my tyres seemed louder than usual as I cycled slowly up the street. The night was still, but a slight breeze was rising, rustling the leaves of the giant copper beeches near at hand. There was no other sound except the distant call of a curlew, and the soft rushing swish of a wind charger, like the beating of unseen wings, up there in the darkness, on the top of old de Lacy's tower, where the jackdaws nested among the ivy. It was producing power from the wind. Something de Lacy never foresaw. The black velvety night wrapped the sleeping village as in a blanket. It made me feel sleepy too. I looked at my watch in the light of my bicycle lamp. It was nearly twelve o'clock and time for me, too, to turn in . Night had fallen on Delvin. "Night with its train of stars, and its great gift of sleep".

Room In The Heart

My native air went to my head like wine when I stepped out of the Granard bus at Maypole. I have, alas, no parents now but I have good friends there who welcomed me. "Where there is room in the heart there is room in the house," is profoundly true. Some days previously, when writing as usual in my little study in Dublin, I sprang up suddenly and said to myself, "I am tired of four walls and a ceiling. I have need of the grass." It was the old call of the country. I knew it well. It never fails to come to me every year in the summertime, the call to return to that spot to which my heart is anchored forever, the place where I was born. I am not alone in feeling the pull of home. The same call comes every year to the countryman or woman who from choice or necessity lives in the city, but it comes more intensely - to some than to others.

I have never been able to resist it. But it is not the same as the urge that sends so many people abroad every year to spend a holiday out of Ireland. It is something far more fundamental than that. It is a profound desire to return to one's roots.

"Fairest on Earth"

I have seen the mighty range of the Swiss Alps from a hundred miles away in France, a long line of snow white peaks and summits high up in the sky, glittering in the sun above the clouds. I have viewed Paris in the springtime from the top of the majestic Arc de Triomphe, the great Arch of the Star, built to the glory of Napoleon, and I have looked down upon the twelve long tree-lined avenues that radiate from it in all directions like the spokes of a wheel and said to myself: "This, surely, is the Queen of Cities, the fairest on the earth."

But I never feel that hunger of the heart to see those world-famous sights again year after year, as I do to lie on the soft summer grass in the breezy sunshine on the top of that lovely green hill, The Ben of Fore, which rises above the old house where I was born.

And the reason is that those wondrously beautiful and faraway mountains and cities hold no dear memories for me, like the memories that cling to every stone and gate and stile around the home of my childhood.

Why, the little cold and bubbling spring well of Boher-na-Kippeen, from which I used to carry a bucket of water to keep the butter cool in summer for my mother is for me, and will ever remain, the magic Fountain of Perpetual Youth.

The Rusting Scythe

Up the winding boreen I wandered slowly along, watching all the changes in field, and hedge and tree. Here was a long hedge of whitethorn quicks that I once held in a bundle in my arms, as my father planted them one by one.

Now the whole hedge was so high that it nearly shut out the daylight along the boreen. All these years while I had been so long away these whitehorns were silently growing, and now they had changed the whole face of the landscape that I knew.

And now my old home is in view. It is deserted now, for the new owners have built a modern house higher up, and "lonely I wander through scenes of my childhood." Out in the barn my father's scythe still hangs rusty from the rafters, the keen blade worn thin with many years of mowing. He himself has long fallen before the Scythe of the greatest Reaper of all.

Measuring Mark

Here is the once cosy kitchen where we were all so happy in the firelight long ago. There is the same mark in the chimney-post about three feet from the ground where I used to measure how far up I could reach. I could see again the tiny fingernails of the child I was then, stretching upwards trying to reach that mark - and here I am now looking down at it.

I am presently standing alone in the square low-ceilinged bedroom where I was born and I look through the small thick-walled window that let in the cold November daylight on that first mysterious day of my existence.

It was from this small room that I set forth on the great one-way journey of Life. It was in this quiet, lamp-lit room, while still a child, but getting used to sorrow, that I watched a much-loved young mother, after prolonged suffering, pass to Heaven, leaving me here alone, never to know a mother's love again in this world.

Swans of Lir

I must not let my thoughts linger on those things now. I must go out quickly and climb my own beloved hill, and distract my mind with the sunlit glories of the view from the summit. There I will find "the medicine for heartache that lurks in lovely things."

It is so green and restful in the sunny quietness of a summer day. A few sheep and an occasional goat nibble at the grass. The rabbits have also discovered it lately, but it has not been discovered by the crowd, nor is it ever likely to be.

I look around me and can see half Ireland from Wicklow to Tipperary. Slane of St. Patrick and the cairn-crowned Loughcrew Hills of Blessed Oliver Plunkett are all in view. Lough Derrevaragh of the Swans of Lir, a long blue shield of water, washes the foot of Knockeyon.

Gem of Lakes

Lough Sheelin peeps out, like a shining sword from behind the bare height of Mullach Maol and laps the little fields of Cavan. Louth Lene, the gem of the Westmeath lakes, with its lovely green wooded islands set in dark blue water, is at my feet.

Little winding silver rivers wander in and out among them all through fields of incredible green and bogs of incredible brown.

It was from this lovely landscape that my dear brother, the late Michael Walsh, derived the title for his first book of poems, "Brown Earth and Green."

Glories of Fore

Deep in the valley beneath the hill lies the modern village of Fore, dominated by the magnificent ruin of the great abbey once raised here to the glory of God. Even in ruin and decay, its stately towers and turreted battlements, its three lovely Romanesque chancel windows, and above all, its exquisitely carved cloister arches, are still beautiful as a "wreck of Paradise."

Gables of ancient churches, broken walls and massive town gates, holy wells and weather-worn stone crosses are all that remain to tell the story of the olden glories of Fore.

But now the summer evening is drawing to a close, and I have not noticed the passing of time. I could dream and linger here for hours, and whenever I revisit my native hill I always feel that time is too short and that "life slips by like a fieldmouse, not shaking the grass."

Dreams of Morning

Down in the valley, too, there is the charm of old neighbours talking to me slowly and saying good-bye over half-doors, telling me as they scrutinize my face, how, each year, I am growing more and more to resemble some long-dead man or woman of my kindred.

There is the great joy of forgetting for a little while the troubles of life while wandering at will through the fields and paths of childhood, and lingering at the rustic styles that knew my morning dreams.

"The little cares that fretted me,
I lost them yesterday.
The fears of what may come to pass,
I cast them all away
Among the clover-scented grass
Among the new-mown hay.
I lost them in green fields of corn,
Where bright red poppies nod
Where ill thoughts die and good are born,
Out in the fields with God."

Down the Old Bog Road with Teresa Brayton

When I first heard the famous Irish ballad "The Old Bog Road" I concluded that the poet had in mind some remembered boreen leading to a bog in Co. Wexford.

Perhaps the mention of "Ferns Church" had something to do with this. I remember many summers ago visiting that ancient Wexford town, and inquiring the whereabouts of the Old Bog Road.

Sunning himself on a low wall I saw a grey-bearded old man. "Oh yes", he said, in answer to my question, and pointing with his stick. "About two miles down that road, and turn to your right at the second cross-roads".

"Is that the road the song was made about?" "Oh yes", said he, "That's the very road", and as I thanked him and left he began to lilt in a quavering voice the first line: "My feet are here on Broadway this blessed harvest morn..."

Old boreen

After an hour's brisk walking I found an old boreen all right, leading to a swamp, but something told me that this was not the poet's "Old Bog road".

Years afterwards I met Teresa Brayton, the author of that old song, in a friend's house in Dublin, and told her of my fruitless journey. It made her laugh heartily, and she said to me: "That old bog road has been located in Kerry and again in Donegal, but sometime you must come down to Kilbrook, near Enfield, where I was born, and I will show you the place I had in mind when writing the ballad in New York".

I found Teresa Brayton shy and reserved when in a crowded room. She was at home only with those who shared her interests, but if one were interested in poetry or the arts she asked no more.

Wonderful memory

She had a richly-stored mind and was "never less alone than when alone". She had a wonderful memory for poetry and could recite countless little poems by heart in her rich, resonant voice, and many a winter's night I sat enthralled listening to her at her cosy fireside in her little flat in Dublin.

Out of the many I heard, I remember one little lyric of which she was very fond and used to recite so often that I memorised it myself. I do not know who wrote it, and neither did she.

She loved flowers and her home in Kilbrook was a bower of roses in the summer. Maybe this was partly the reason why the poem appealed to her so much.

Red Geraniums

Life did not bring me silken gowns
Nor jewels for my hair,
Nor signs of gabled foreign towns
In distant countries fair.
But I can glimpse beyond my pane
A green and friendly hill
And red geraniums aflame
Upon my window-sill.
The brambled cares of every day
The tiny humdrum things
May bind my feet when they would stray
But still my heart has wings.
While red geraniums are bloomed
Against my window glass
And low above my green-sweet hill
The gipsy wind-clouds pass.
And if my dreamings ne'er come true
The brightest and the best
But leave me lone my journey through
I'll set my heart at rest.
And thank God for home-sweet things,
A green and friendly hill

And red geraniums aflame
Upon my window-sill.

Time passed and Teresa Brayton returned to her old home near Enfield to end her days in peace.

Warm Welcome

One harvest day in 1941, I received a letter in her vigorous handwriting inviting me down to Kilbrook.

Her health was failing at the time, but she gave me a warm welcome in her rose-covered cottage on the side of the road just outside the village.

Small in stature, she was dressed in a gay floral frock. Her bobbed silver hair framed a calm face, the most striking feature of which was her bright alert eyes.

When tea was over she said, "Now I am going to show you the Old Bog Road".

We strolled together up the main Dublin road for about a quarter of a mile, talking all the while of poets and their songs.

Suddenly she stopped where a long boreen branched off to the left, and pointed down it with her walking stick. "That", said she, "is the old bog road leading into the bog of Cappagh, where I spent many a happy day when I was young. It was of that old boreen I was thinking when I was writing the song".

We walked a little way together down towards the bog, and fearing of tiring her too much I suggested that we turn back.

She leaned on my arm heavily as we turned and I was profoundly moved, as I had a premonition that I would never see her alive again.

But it is a memory that I will always cherish - that I walked arm-in-arm with Teresa Brayton down the Old Bog Road.

Flowering Primroses

It was a sunny St. Patrick's Day in the early years of World War I. Frank Reilly had the day free, and was gazing aimlessly across the green level acres of the Curragh. He had been kept busy all the week serving out cups of tea, bovril and cakes to the soldiers, who kept continually coming in and out of the canteen where he worked.

But yesterday the regiment had left for France. He had watched them march away, fine young men, to a war not of their making, and from which the majority of them were destined never to return. And now the camp was deserted - only a few stray sheep scattered here and there, like grey boulders.

It was his twenty-third birthday and Frank felt a sudden feeling of loneliness surge up in him. He wanted to talk to somebody, and the thought came to him that he would cycle over to Castlebrowne to see his old friend, Jimmy Bracken, who worked in the grocery shop and publichouse of Peter Scally, the richest man in the village.

He and Jimmy had worked together before, and had become fast friends, mainly through a common interest, a love of books and reading. This shared interest set them apart from the usual type of grocer's assistant, whose main concern was with racing, football and the dogs.

Frank and Jimmy cared for none of those things. On their free days they used to go for long rambles together through the lanes and fields of Castlebrowne, their talk being of books and poetry and the "light that never was on sea or land". Needless to say, their colleagues of the dog-racing type who had no use for books considered them "a little mad".

Often in their rambles together the subject of love and marriage cropped up, and both were unanimous in their decision that the respective girls of their heart must, in addition to being good housewives, share their tastes for the delight of books. Jimmy was

187

a bit of a poet also and used to write verses for the local paper, in the precious intervals stolen from serving the thirsty souls of the village.

Frank enjoyed every mile of the journey as the day was lovely and calm. Rounding a corner of the road near the village, he saw a group of young men and girls sitting on the low wall of the little Castlebrowne bridge. He recognised them as pals of Jimmy Bracken, and they hailed him noisily.

One girl whom he did not know remained sitting demurely on the bridge. He had just noted the dark ripple of hair over her temples, the wide, good-natured mouth and smiling, blue eyes, when Willie Dowling called out to her:
"This is Frank Reilly, Molly, a friend of Jimmy Bracken's - up in Scally's, you know - Molly Kearney".

During the conversation with Jimmy Bracken, later in the evening, he confided to Frank that he was shortly to be married, and rather self-consciously produced a photograph of his fiancee for Frank's inspection. Frank did not see any particular charm in the lady, but made a few polite remarks about the picture, and then blurted out rather abruptly:

"Does she read?"
"Well", Jimmy explained, "she has not much time. She is a nurse to Major Blake's children up at Stonestown, and she finds her whole time taken up with the work".

Jimmy had always maintained hitherto that the girl he would marry must be a lover of books, like himself, and now here he was finding excuses for her indifference to the printed page. Oh, well, love did strange things to a man.

As he cycled back to the Curragh that evening he found himself wondering if the girl with the black ripple of hair, the sunny smile and the wide, good-natured mouth was a lover of books.

Two years passed away before he met her again, this time in Dublin. He was elbowing his way through a crowd at the

188

Kingsbridge station when he saw her slim figure struggling with a suit-case. He knew her at once, a curl of her dark hair escaping from under the brim of a chic little hat, the pleasant, good-natured face, the smiling blue eyes.

"Pardon me, aren't you Miss Kearney?"
She looked puzzled for a moment, and slowly she recognised him.
"You are Mr. Reilly?"
"Call me Frank", he said impulsively, "and give me that suit-case".

She admired the masterful way he made a lane for her through the crowd, the way he made things easy for her as he lifted the heavy case into the bus, and would not leave her until he had extracted a promise from her that she would meet him again.

And that was how it began. One meeting led to another, then he took her to the pictures and to an occasional dance and theatre, and in the bright, Summer days he would take her for long walks in the country. Frank had the poet's love for the open air, and liked to linger in the green fields. By dint of seeing each other continually, their friendship ripened into love, and soon they both found out that they were indispensable to each other.

Though Frank occasionally remembered a rather cynical saying he had read somewhere "Be sure to get what you like, or you will begin to like what you get", he paid no heed to it, and the fact that Molly was not particularly interested in the things of the mind was nothing compared to the feeling she had inspired in him.

It was on St. Patrick's Day he proposed to her. They were together visiting her mother's home in Castlebrowne, and they were walking slowly and happily down by the river bank and through the little fields. The March sky was blue, the sun was shining, and the young lambs ran races up and down the sunny side of the old hawthorn hedge. The grass beneath was starred with primroses, in rich yellow profusion, making a brightness everywhere. It was there in the midst of the lambs and primroses that he gave her the engagement ring, and they kissed and were happy together.

In twelve months they were married, and two years later their first baby was born. And it was then that Frank began to realise that the advent of the baby was of far more importance to his wife that all his books. Hitherto his love for her had blinded him to the fundamental fact that she was not interested in his literary tastes. She could not share in his appreciation of a fine line of poetry - the beauty of the chiselled phrase.

But of course, he told himself it was too much to expect. One could not have everything. Her heart was centred in the baby and him, she delighted in keeping the home bright and cheerful, she was a splendid cook, and was always spotless and ready to wait on him when he would come home tired from the office. She was a perfect wife, if she would only take an interest in his books and his poetry.

He often chaffed her about it, and told her she had no soul, but she retorted good-humouredly:
"How would you like to come home some evening and no tea ready, and find me reading a book?"

Against such an argument what was he to say. And yet he was conscious of a secret feeling of disappointment that he did not marry a woman who in addition to her housewifery qualities could enter with him into the delights of the mind, "the realms of gold".

The years flew by, and other children were born to them and grew up, and soon would come the silver jubilee of their marriage. All these years Frank had tried to forget his disappointment and became more absorbed that ever in his beloved books.

Molly, for her part, although quite happy, always secretly wondered if Frank's love for her was as deep as she knew hers was for him. In one of his books which she had opened at random, he came upon the lines of a poem, "Man's love is of man's life a thing apart, 'tis woman's whole existence", and it perturbed her, for she felt instinctively it was true.

Frank, for his part, had become resigned to her limitations, but was not blind to her manifold virtues. Good old Molly! What a

190

comfort it was to hear her footsteps downstairs, busy with the housework always at his beck and call! How helpless he would be without her!

He remembered with gratitude her unfailing ministrations during the few times he was ill in their long, married life. How loyally and maternally she watched over him and had special Masses said for his recovery! Not even his mother could have cared for him as she did!

And then one day, when Spring was in the air, and the daffodils in bunches were for sale in the city streets, she came to him and said: "Frank, dear, I'd love to see young lambs and primroses again".

He could not believe his ears. Was this the same Molly who had taken no interest in his poetry, talking about lambs and primroses, the very stuff of poetry? When he recovered from his surprise, he said:
"Why! You do appreciate lambs and primroses! You must have a poetic soul after all! Where was it hidden all these years?"
"Yes", she said, "I want to see young, white lambs with innocent faces".

St. Patrick's Day was a day of blue and gold - a day stolen from Summer, when Frank and Molly set out for the bus that was to take them to Castlebrowne. They queued up early to get the front seat to the left of the driver, where they could have a perfect armchair view of the country, unimpeded by other people's hats or newspapers.

Away to the left the Wicklow Mountains - a long, blue wall - stood out against the sky as the bus raced onward. And now their journey was done. Together they wandered down by the river bank to the old hawthorn hedge. Time had stood still.

The same sun was shining down from the sky of Springtime blue, the same wisps of white cloud were drifting overhead, and most delightful of all, masses of delicate yellow primroses peeping out from their rough green leaves starred the grass under the hawthorns. On a little hillock of close-cropped grass nearby four or five white lambs were playing in the sun. All around them was the eternal changelessness of Nature, ever young, just as it was twenty-five years ago.

"Nothing has changed", she breathed rapturously, "except us, we have grown old".

Frank saw her again as she looked on that long-past day, flushed and smiling, the dark, rippling hair, the wide, good-humoured mouth.

"Our hearts have not changed", he said softly, as he kissed her and began to lilt "Though your hair has turned to silver I will love you just the same".

"Oh, Frank, we will come here every year at primrose-time", she cried impulsively.

"Yes", he answered slowly, "we will come here every year as long as we live!"

His unspoken thought was: "There won't be many years left".

Molly intuitively divined what he was thinking, for she was very silent as they took their seats in the bus for home. She was still silent when Frank squeezed her arm.

"A penny for your thoughts, Molly".

She turned to him wistfully.

"I was just wondering if there will be lambs and primroses in the fields of Heaven".

Frank was about to laugh but he checked himself. After all, he would humour her fancy. She was still a child in many ways, even though her hair was white. After a pause, he said gently:

"Well, Molly dear, I am not sure about the primroses, but I do know the Lamb of God will be there".

"Of course, that is true", she murmured reflectively, more to herself than to him, "and wherever He is, everything beautiful will be there too, so there are sure to be primroses".

A happy, thoughtful silence fell between them as the bus sped back to the city.